How I Fired My Boss & Made More Money

INSIDER SECRETS

from Successful
Interim Executives and
Independent Consultants

Kristen McAlister & Pamela Wasley

INDIE BOOKS
INTERNATIONAL

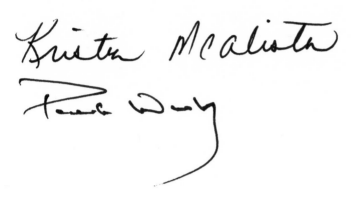

ISBN-10: 1-941870-81-3
ISBN-13: 978-1-941870-81-5
Library of Congress Control Number: 2017932735

Designed by Joni McPherson, mcphersongraphics.com

INDIE BOOKS INTERNATIONAL, LLC
2424 VISTA WAY, SUITE 316
OCEANSIDE, CA 92054

www.indiebooksintl.com

CONTENTS

PREFACE

We have been educating, advising, and placing independent executives for more than a decade. We often step back and wonder how two people who have never worked in a big four consulting firm or the staffing industry ended up owning an interim executive and management consulting company. Our experiences are from both the client and the executive perspective. We both come from backgrounds working inside companies in various industries at various stages of growth. We have worked side-by-side with CEOs and owners to grow their businesses. We have also been independent executives growing a business of one.

For Pamela, after a few years of consulting on her own, she joined forces with a few other consultants and started referring business amongst the group. After a while, two big challenges existed. First, when everyone was busy, there was little business development being done. Second, most were not very good at marketing or business development, so only a select few were bringing in the leads. In an effort to resolve these two challenges, a business was born. The company was the marketing and business development arm and referral source for the consultants. Not the only source, but a viable one.

Over the next few years, the company transitioned from consulting to an interim executive-focused company. The challenge then became a lack of familiarity with this term in the marketplace. It couldn't even be found in any career drop-downs. There were variations, such as "Consultant," or "Business Coach," but never "Interim Executive". The marketplace existed, and the need was there, but it never really stood out as a career choice. Years later, there still isn't an option for it in a drop-down, but more than ever there is a growing population of executives who are working independently.

It is this independent executive whom we get the pleasure to work with on a daily basis and have now for a combined twenty years. Through these conversations, we have gained insights, seen trends, and counseled thousands of executives on the subject of growing their independent executive business. On the flip side, we have also talked to and worked with thousands of companies and business owners.

Based on this perspective, we end up answering questions from executives who are either actively growing their business or looking to transition. The conversations range from questions about how to position themselves in the marketplace to getting more clients. We have always been willing to share our experiences and knowledge. The overwhelming quantity and range of these questions are what prompted us to finally put it all on paper in one place.

This is not a set of formulas, but a collection of experiences, guidelines, and stories anyone can leverage and apply to his or her unique situation.

Whether an executive is considering a move to being independent or has been independent for more decades than they care to admit, learning never ends. As much as some may enjoy learning from their own experiences, it is always helpful when you can learn from someone else's as well.

Kristen McAlister

Pamela Wasley

January 2017

SECTION I

Why is Building a Successful Business of One Such a Mystery?

CHAPTER 1

What Successful Competitors Won't Tell You

J ames had a successful career as an executive. He spent most of the past fifteen years primarily in an operational role working with a couple of companies in the consumer goods industry. His degree and early career were in computer science and IT. As a COO, he has typically been responsible for IT as well as overall operations. His last two positions were eliminated when the companies were purchased. After going through it the second time, he decided to make a change. James took his collective experience and went to work independently as an executive. He updated his LinkedIn page, came up with a company name, had business cards printed, and started letting people know he was available for work on an interim, part-time, or consulting basis. He could help middle-market companies identify and implement breakthrough growth opportunities, taking them to the next level of performance.

James began by attending networking functions, meeting potential referral partners for coffee here and there, and signing up with every website he could find that worked with interim executives, management consultants, or advisors.

After about four months, James became frustrated. He had met with a grand total of four potential clients and had done one small assessment for a company. A few months later, he met with a few more potential clients and was working with one client three days a month while also helping a few startups get to the point of funding. Unfortunately, the startups weren't in a position to pay James yet. James had heard about the flexibility being independent gave you, he just wished his schedule wasn't *this* flexible.

The next two years were a bit of a struggle, but James did gain some traction. He was able to keep busy about two days a week for at least nine months of the year and making about one-half of what he had in his last corporate job. That wasn't too bad since he was only working 30 percent of the time. Still, he had thought at this point he would be working more and making at least the same as he had when he was full time, with the flexibility of only working three to four days a week. What was he missing?

Denise had a similar career to James's. She worked with a number of companies in an executive role for the last fifteen years and had her last couple of positions eliminated, either due to acquisition or company relocation. With children still at home, she made the decision not to relocate them. Instead, she decided to create a career that gave her more control and the availability to be with her family as needed. Denise decided to be an independent executive. Denise did a lot of the same things James did to build her business, but with a few differences. Two years later, Denise is turning down business because she either doesn't have the availability or she isn't excited about the engagement.

With such similar backgrounds and situations, why is Denise in the position of turning business away while James is still doing everything he can to keep busy at least half the time? This is the million-dollar question.

We talk to thousands of independent executives every year. The number one question we are asked is, "How can I get more visibility to grow my business?" We have watched some executives struggle, and we have seen others who are in such high demand that they are able to name their price and clients will pay it. We do know, however, that money is not always the number one driving force for independent executives. The driving force and interpretation of "success" vary greatly, from keeping a full schedule of clients, receiving a higher than usual hourly rate to creating immense value for clients. In each of these cases, increased income is typically the result. However you interpret success, we will share with you some of the top secrets of successful independent executives and how they got there.

Throughout this book, we will share stories and examples. Though most will be told through proxies such as James and Denise, they are a compilation of our firsthand experiences. We will also repeat some advice in different chapters, both for emphasis and because we want readers to be able to pick up the book and turn to whichever topic is most relevant and pressing at the moment.

The Modern IC Marketplace

Work arrangements in the United States are shifting swiftly away from what we think of as the traditional model of work—a full-time, permanent position with a single employer. An alternative model of independent contracting (IC) is on the rise, driven by economic reasons and lifestyle preferences that demand greater flexibility.

In recent decades, we see more and more workers opting to work independently, on a project-by-project basis. Today's professionals place a high enough premium on autonomy that they are willing to strike out on their own, even as the United States tax system, health care system, and other infrastructure are slow to catch up. And even though it means forfeiting certain fundamental employer-provided benefits, such as healthcare, retirement packages, and built-in professional development.

The recent rise in independent contracting has been accompanied by a rising demand for interim talent. More and more employers are integrating contingent workers into their operational strategy.

Technological advances and intermediary platforms have been instrumental in allowing companies to tap into specialized skills and know-how on an as-needed basis. This flexibility in talent management is shown to cut costs and drive innovation by allowing companies to take more risks; being able to test a new business idea with a $500,000 "get it going fast and let's see" model, rather than a fully drawn $5 million business plan with commitments to permanent staff, would ultimately enable them to find more promising opportunities.

The demands of a globalized economy, greater connectivity through technology, and the shift towards more flexibility for employer and employee alike are all factors altering work arrangements in the United States.

The History of the IC Marketplace

If we look at the history of the American workforce, we see that independent contracting is far from a recent phenomenon. In fact, it predates our traditional model of full-time permanent employment.

In pre-industrial society, Americans worked for themselves as artisans, farmers, and small shopkeepers. During the late-nineteenth-century manufacturing era, big companies still outsourced their labor, and turnover was high (300 percent)[1]. Then increasingly complex industrial machinery led to a more stable, trained workforce. As workers became concentrated in cities and industrial hubs, workers' unions formed to demand higher pay and better conditions. During World War II, wage and price controls forced employers to begin offering benefits and pension plans in order to reward and retain their workers. This is when our modern model of full-time permanent employment came into full swing.

Independent contracting came back on the scene when companies were forced to downsize during the 1970s and

---

[1] https://hbr.org/2012/05/the-rise-of-the-supertemp

1980s recession; then came globalization and technological advances, making it easier to offshore production and knowledge work overseas. Finally, the 2007 recession brought about a full resurgence of the independent professional. Digital technology has made it possible to develop a spot market for high-end talent and drive transaction costs down.

In light of the recent resurgence, companies are beginning to re-envision which skills and resources belong inside versus outside the organization. The relationship between employer and employee is undergoing yet another transformation.

The Future of the IC Marketplace

Today's independent contracting market is not expected to slow down, and employers are expected to get more creative with their operational decisions. Studies increasingly confirm the benefits of flexible work arrangements. A 2013 Columbia University study[2] shows a strong correlation in today's economy between high-performing companies and flexible talent management:

> [C]ompanies that successfully carried out process or production innovations displayed higher levels of non-traditional employment models—including contracting, part-time, freelance and temporary workers.

As health coverage becomes more portable and legislation catches up, independent contracting will go from being

---

[2] http://docplayer.net/6629303-Independent-contracting-policy-and-management-analysis.html

an appealing work arrangement to an increasingly *realistic* arrangement for more and more Americans. It is expected that workers will only continue to desire autonomy and a better work-life balance in their lives.

As baby-boomers retire, the demand for talent will rise. Companies will find resources on the open market to be increasingly reliable and accessible, especially as their internal operations adjust to better accommodate them.

A 2016 presentation by NERA Economic Consulting[3] outlines a company's economic reasons for choosing alternative work arrangements. The independent contractor marketplace allows employers to achieve:

- Increased efficiency through a project-based workflow

- Greater agility in responding to fluctuating demand

- Better performance through output-based compensation

- Lower costs through employee-owned assets

According to the *Harvard Business Review*[4], today's professionals—including executives, consultants, lawyers and other high-end talent—are without a doubt moving towards alternative work arrangements:

> [O]ur experience suggests that if talented people knew they could leave their permanent posts and get both a reliable flow of interesting, challeng-

---

[3] http://www.nera.com/content/dam/nera/publications/2016/Independent_Contracting_Presentation_v2_022916.pdf

[4] https://hbr.org/2012/05/the-rise-of-the-supertemp

ing, well-paid projects *and* group health coverage, traditional firms would see a mass exodus. Chances are good that those two aspirations will be widely achievable in the United States within a decade.

It is certain that state and federal legislatures need to update tax laws and more clearly define the differences between independent contractors and employees. But as the benefits of the independent contractor marketplace—for employers, employees and the economy as a whole—become more and more evident, policy is bound to catch up.

The Rise of the Executive Temp

As mentioned, a number of factors has caused an increase in former corporate executives offering their services to companies on a temporary or project basis. It can be debated whether these executives are part of a growing career category referred to as independent executives or simply joining hundreds of thousands of other small business owners. Either way, no longer does an executive need to spend countless hours working for the same company year after year, only to have most of the total accomplishments achieved in year one. Nor does a CEO or business owner need to spend months looking for the perfect candidate to fill a range of needs over the next couple of years to then have the executive peak within the first year or not work out at all. The speed of business in today's market is pushing the need for quicker decisions, shorter timelines, and immediate results. There is no one-size-fits-all in the executive suite. As a result, we are seeing a shift from needing to own an executive's expertise for a number of years to simply leasing expertise on an as-needed basis. We see top-level executives enjoying long and accomplished careers as independent executives.

What Does "Independent Executive" Cover?

It seems as though there are almost as many terms used to describe various types of independent executives as there are words for water in the Hawaiian language. Many of these are driven by the marketplace and perceptions. Since many of the underlying principles of how executives market and sell their services are the same, we use the term *independent executive* to refer to the full spectrum of ways executives contract with clients. Here are a few examples of popular terms and how they are typically applied.

Part-time/Fractional

An engagement that occupies fewer than five days per week. A part-time executive role is typically one to three days per week and can last for up to a year or more. This is common in the area of finance and marketing. Companies do not have the budget nor the need for a full-time executive in these roles but certainly need some executive-level expertise. The need is ongoing and the role is likely needed until the company grows to the point of justifying the full-time cost. For example:

- A company lacks the financial expertise to grow without taking unnecessary risks: A part-time CFO will have the right expertise to give leadership the ability to make the right decisions for the company.

Interim/Temporary Executive

The terms *interim* and *temporary* are often used interchangeably. They usually refer to an engagement in which the executive is needed five days a week for a short duration. This is most common when an executive is brought in to fill a gap between the departure of one key executive and the start date of a new executive, there is an initiative requiring hands-on expertise and management that is missing from that company, or the current executive team does not have any bandwidth left to accomplish the initiative. For example:

- A company is experiencing rapid growth and the infrastructure is starting to collapse. Most of the management team that started with the company has been promoted more for tenure than for ability or expertise. While the CEO concentrates on continuing the growth, an interim President or COO can put in more flexible and scalable infrastructure so the organization can withstand the rapid growth.

Consulting/Project

An executive is brought in to complete a specific task, often an assessment or planning. It is typically completed within a short timeframe. This is a great option for companies to fill an expertise gap, execute a strategic plan, project, or test the waters with someone new. For example:

- The CEO knows the company could be run more efficiently and that profits should be higher. An operations consultant can come in and quickly assess the company and determine not just where and what, but how, and lay out a plan that leverages internal resources. Many times, he or she finds low-hanging fruit that brings immediate savings to the bottom line and will work with the internal team to achieve those results.

Board Director/Advisor

The executive's expertise is of great value to the company and is available as needed to provide insights. This can be done ad-hoc or during regular meetings. For example:

- A company has been stagnant the past few years and is not meeting its yearly goals. Every company goes through this stage at one time or another. A board member from a similar, but different industry can bring a fresh perspective to a company's strategy to get it growing again.

Coaching

This can easily be an industry in itself. Since the nature of the work is well defined and does not include being hands-on in the organization, it is often structured and perceived as an advisory role. There are a number of certifications and trainings for business coaching, which lend more structure to the industry than most of the categories above.

Many independent executives have struggled for years trying to figure out whether to brand themselves as an interim executive, consultant, advisor, fractional executive, etc. Most executives can easily step into any of these roles. We have seen an increase in the use of the term "portfolio career" used to describe this.

The terminology is often marketplace driven. Though many can debate whether there is a difference between an interim executive engagement and a consulting engagement, the only perspective that matters is that of the marketplace. What term(s) is the target customer base most likely to use? If there is any uncertainty, then it comes down to a branding decision for the executive. Does the executive want to make the distinction? If so, what type of work does the executive want to target, i.e. interim, project, advisory, etc.? The more focused it is, the more the executive is likely to be remembered and referred. We will cover this in more detail in chapter 2.

The Independent Executive

We have seen executive careers take many forms over the past decade. Some career transformation was caused by economic changes, while other times it was influenced by personal changes. Experienced executives have a number of options when making the next career choice: taking a full-time position, retiring, focusing on board work, or going independent as a contingent executive, i.e., interim executive, management consultant, advisor, or coach.

As much as each of these decisions seemed independent of the other, during the past decade, we have witnessed executive careers as more fluid, interchanging, and often overlapping among these options. Working with executives who primarily want to work on a contingent basis has offered us many insights over the past ten years. We often receive inquiries surrounding what that career choice looks like, what an executive can expect, and why executives choose this path. According to survey data from our 2016 research report, "The Independent Executive,"[5] there are some consistencies among interim executives and independent consultants when it comes to income expectations, building a practice, and delivering value to clients.

Who Makes Up the Independent Executive Workforce?

With over 75 percent of the executives surveyed being baby boomers, it is clear that being independent isn't just for a retired executive who isn't ready to play golf full-time. We are seeing more executives step into this kind of career long before they are near retirement age. They have had successful executive careers and are now looking to work independently with various companies who can use their expertise.

There is a growing demand for interim executives at the CEO and President level. There are a number of variables that affect the top position depending on whether it is family owned, privately owned, or publicly traded. From retirement to health issues and even predecessors being forced out, the increased demand is reflected in our survey, with more than 45 percent of interim executives providing top-level

[5] https://ceriusexecutives.com/interim-executive-confidential-independent-executive-4/

expertise. This is closely followed by operations, at 41.3 percent. We were surprised to see technology expertise more predominantly represented than finance with more than 21 percent of those polled. Finance, sales, and marketing were somewhat close, ending up between 17 and 18 percent.

Why Does an Executive Do Interim or Management Consulting Work?

It was clear from our survey that independent executives love the freedom of this type of work. It provides a better work/life balance than their previous careers, along with the ability to choose the types of challenges they want. There was also a strong pull for this independent lifestyle for those in the process of looking for their next role (permanent or temporary) and executives who have sold their companies or are semi-retired. As most executives enjoy the freedom of independent executive work, more than 86 percent said they would consider a full-time position for the right opportunity. This is down from 90 percent in 2013, based on the preference to remain independent, which supports the results that more than 90 percent would recommend interim or consulting work to another executive.

Over the past ten years, we have seen executive careers become more fluid between independent executives and full-time employed roles than the prior decades. It is no longer one or the other. As we track executive careers over the past decade, we are seeing less of a division and more of a migration from one to the other, depending on a number of variables from personal situations, external factors, and the need for either consistency or variability at any given point. At the same time, the average tenure of a company executive has shortened quite a bit, causing some to question how long is "long-term employment."

What Does Their Business Look Like?

Most independent executives spend much of their time doing business development and securing opportunities. Though the independent executive concept is being adopted by more and more companies in the United States, there is still a percentage of the SMB (small and medium-sized business) market unaware that this option exists. When asked about their top sources for securing engagements, the executives in our survey said networking was at the top of their list at 84.7 percent, with referrals coming in second at 62.8 percent. However, the Internet is fast becoming a substantial resource for many independent executives. From online talent marketplaces to social media, more than 36 percent of the executives use the Internet as an effective source for opportunities.

Though there is an extensive range of remuneration rates for independent executives, more than 70 percent of the executives reported client rates between $100 and 250 per hour, with the median at $150 to 200 per hour. There does not seem to be a connection between a lower or higher rate and the amount of time an executive has been working independently. For example, there is no correlation between what an executive who has been independent for one year charges per hour compared to those who have been independent for five years. Their rates do not seem to go up based on time as an independent executive.

How busy an independent executive is depends primarily on two factors: how busy he or she wants to be, and how long he or she has been developing the independent executive business. Some key points:

- Just over 50 percent of the respondents had worked at least two days a week on an engagement in the last two years.

- On the flip side, just under 30 percent had worked less than one day per week.

- This coincides with just over 30 percent having had been independent executives for less than one year. There is a correlation between how long executives are independent and how many days per week they are working. For most, it takes time to develop their businesses to keep a consistent pipeline of leads and opportunities for engagements. The amount of time this takes to build, including the amount of time on a weekly and monthly basis, is one of the factors we see driving the online talent marketplaces.

- Regardless of how much an executive is working, work/life balance is clearly seen, with more than 72 percent of executive respondents taking off three or more weeks per year. That is defined as no client work, no networking, and no business development.

As quickly as the weather can change, so can the life and career of an executive. The good news is, an executive's career now comes in every shape and size, from corporate executive, business owner, startup entrepreneur, interim executive, management consultant, coach, advisor, board member, and the list goes on.

Is Being an Independent Executive the Right Career Path for You?

We mentioned a number of ways an independent executive can work with and make an impact for companies and leaders. Any of these can offer a great amount of flexibility, financial freedom, and challenges as an alternative career choice to being a fully employed executive for a single company. Many executives see working as an independent executive more as building a business of one (or solopreneur) rather than simply working independently. This can be a challenging decision, starting with whether growing an independent executive business is the right choice for you.

As mentioned, most executives choose this career for one of three reasons: freedom of the work, a gap while looking for their next full-time role, or semi-retirement/just sold their company and transitioning out of a full-time role.

Freedom of the Work

"Freedom" is prone to interpretation and depends on your perspective, particularly for independent executives. What we hear most is that they enjoy the challenge of working with a variety of companies with varying levels of needs and challenges. Most tend to get bored easily, so a new challenge offers a great amount of stimulation, and once the situation has stabilized or goals are accomplished, the executive is ready to transition.

It is easy to question how much freedom an independent executive actually has. The executive is either scheduled out with networking events trying to get the business or is tied up with clients once he or she gets the business. As true as this is, the executive still has the ultimate decision about which events to attend, as well as how many and which clients and situations to take on. The workload can then be adjusted as personal and professional situations change.

Using Denise as the example, she only takes engagements up to four days a week with no travel, since she is very involved in coaching her children's soccer teams. At one point, she decided to invest her time in developing part of her toolkit into a technology suite and was available only one to two days per week. As that was launched and until revenues came in, she then started taking on more engagements. Other executives we have worked with enjoy taking three- to six-month engagements working five to six days per week, then take the next couple of months off.

What type of freedom you want and how much of it can affect the type of work an executive decides to pursue.

Looking for the Next Role

It is not uncommon for executives to look at doing some interim executive or management consulting project work while they look for their next full-time role. It became more common during the recent economic recovery for executives to use this model as a foot in the door. It then continued as a means for executives to test the waters for their next position. Using the Project-to-Perm model, they will start an engagement on a contract basis then transition to a full-time employee at some point. Think of this as foresight for both the executive and the company. Experienced executives have a good idea at this point in their careers what types of companies and roles they enjoy and want to take. It is always challenging to make a decision to accept an employment offer based on research and interviews. This model gives the executive hands-on experience with the company, the position, and expectations prior to accepting a full-time employment offer. We'll discuss this concept more fully later in this chapter.

Semi-Retired or Sold Company

The two most popular statements we get from this group of executives is, "I'm not ready to retire yet, but I'm also not ready to go back to corporate America full time" and, "I've just sold my company and want to continue working, but don't see myself starting another company or working full-time for someone else." Independent executive work is a great alternative to both situations and why about one-third of the executives we've surveyed are in this category.

Whatever the reason, the good news is that it doesn't need to be a life-changing career decision as it once was. As long as executives can get enough work, they absolutely love it. They have flexibility, they get to pick their jobs, and it gives them more choice in what work they do. It doesn't matter if they are retirement age or in the middle of their career; it can be a great choice for many.

Making the Transition to Being Independent

Many executives are not prepared to be independent. They have mostly worked with established or fully supported companies. They have been surrounded by a team, have had a clear focus on the what the company does and the marketplace they are selling, or get to focus on one key area of the business. Now they need to work as a solopreneur. This can be a difficult shift to make, and the transition is made in a variety of ways. Here are some of the more common scenarios we see when executives are transitioning to this type of work.

Making the Swap

An executive's decision to no longer work as an employee can often be as seamless as transitioning from a W2 to a 1099 in their current company with a reduced scope of responsibilities while actively seeking similar types of roles to diversify their source of income. Some may not need to look any further than other companies in the industry. In other cases, a private equity firm purchases the company the executive is working with and the position winds down; they may decide to bring the executive in as an interim executive to another portfolio company they have invested in. In most cases, the executive is able to transition the full-time role to a defined scope of activities with companies who are already familiar with the executive's work.

A Big Change

Whether by choice, planned or unexpected, the executive is no longer in a full-time role and, rather than join the job-seeker path, they decide to start working independently. The executive has some or no work currently but is working diligently on building their network and, hopefully, a portfolio of clients.

What Do I Do Next?

This situation is similar to the prior scenario, but the executive isn't quite sure what he or she is going to do next. We see this quite a bit with executives who are retiring or selling their companies. Most of their discussions are more focused on whether to fully retire or do some advisory or board work. More and more, we are seeing them connect with other company owners who can use their expertise, allowing them to actively stay involved in companies without owning or being an employee.

— CASE IN POINT —

Making the Transition with Sizzling Success

Shira Harrington spent much of her career in recruiting. At the heart of the 2007-2010 recession, many recruiting firms, including hers, went out of business. For about a year, she worked with another recruiting firm to start their Washington, DC office and she was working from home. Seeing where the market was going and uncertain about her future, necessity became the mother of invention. In addition to recruiting, she wanted to open her own career coaching practice. She got permission from her employer to do it for that business. By the end of the year, she realized, "Wait a second. I can do this on my own," and so she did. Shira realized at the time that she had been unknowingly working toward this goal for about a decade.

When Shira was developing her recruiting book of business, she also chose a slightly different path than her coworkers. Rather than being on the phone and making those fifty prospecting calls a day, she spent her time networking. She attended groups as well as starting her own groups. She wanted to get out there and talk and live where her prospects lived. She wanted to understand what keeps the HR community up at night. She started lunch-and-learns, attended Society for Human Resource Management (SHRM) events, and started to live and breathe the air that HR professionals were living and breathing. Through it all, she started to realize what was keeping them up at night. Employee engagement was becoming a very hot issue, and increasingly so over the years. She listened to what they were doing well, what their challenges were. Then, when generational work came her way, she got another perspective on why employers often have the challenges that they do with recruiting, retaining, and engaging employees.

For years, Shira had been attending HR seminars and working closely with the community. During that time, she heard a speech on multigenerational workforces. Shira was so enthralled by the topic, she asked the speaker to come and present at other HR programs she was involved in. Five years later, she had attended so many of his sessions that Shira was his first call to cover a presentation when he couldn't make it. So, Shira's first presentation on a topic that would end up becoming one of the focal points of her brand was given to a group of general managers for The Ritz-Carlton. She continued to research, improve, and make the presentation her own. Her first big test run turned out to include about eighty colleagues, clients, and business professionals in her network to hear about this "generational thing" that she was doing. Then the phone started to ring, and it didn't stop ringing.

She started doing presentations for staff and eventually for conferences. She began raising her rates, and over time gained a reputation, first within the association community and then among certain companies, as a generational diversity speaker. That opened up a completely new practice area that augmented the coaching and recruiting she was doing because it was all about workforce engagement. Shira had found her heart's passion—creating a highly engaged workforce. And so her brand of *Purposeful Hire* was born.

Shira has worked with thousands of clients, been a keynote speaker at HR conferences, and been interviewed numerous times. She encourages others to tap into their passion for service. Put the money aside. Put the business model aside for just a moment. Who do you want to serve? How do you want to serve them? Why do you want to serve them? We are in a day and age where people don't care how much you know until they know how much you care. People want your authentic self, especially if you are a solo practitioner or a business owner. Nobody wants to be sold. People want to be engaged. They want to know that you care about their needs and you have a unique solution to help them solve their urgent problems.

When you can figure out your passions, why you do what you do, and what drives you to be highly engaged, you will then be able to turn that around and say, "Who has the urgent problems that I am in a unique position to help them solve?"

What to Expect

Being independent is a high-pressure job in any industry. Though an executive is accustomed to working however many hours it takes to get the job done, the focus always used to be on one company, and all of the time was focused there. Now time is split between building a business as well as working with multiple other businesses, often at the same time.

If an executive is someone who needs structure, then he or she will need to think through how to organize the business to give it that structure. Inherently, with a solo practice, there is no structure, and this is tough for most initially. As many independent executives can attest, being independent is not for the weak of heart. It not only takes a variety of skill sets but a cast iron stomach as well to be able to roll with the ups and downs. As much as we discuss the flexibility and life balance this career can offer, there can be some challenges as well.

Choosing this career is starting a business. The executive is now responsible for business development, marketing, sales, IT, operations, accounting, and finance. In many cases, the executive is also the administrative assistant and travel agent. Fortunately, given the technological tools available, this is much easier than it was a decade ago.

Some of the more challenging aspects can be developing a portfolio of clients and meeting the various demands and challenges each client will bring. An executive building the business with little or no base can expect it to be at least a year before acquiring enough quality clients to provide a reasonable source of income. Since interim executive and management consulting work is intended to be temporary, a large part of the focus should be on constantly coming up with ways to better build your pipeline and your business.

A Growing Alternative—Project-to-Perm (a.k.a. Temp-to-Perm, Try Before You Buy)

The lines are starting to blur more and more between an executive who only accepts full-time employment offers and one who is independent and works on a contract basis. This is being driven by both the executive and the company. One business development trend we are seeing goes back to the traditional interim executive model.

As we've mentioned, an executive's career is no longer black-and-white—"I'm an executive in corporate America" versus "I'm a consultant." As clichéd as it is to say, times have changed. The tenure of the average employed executive continues to decrease. It is not uncommon for executives to tell us they view all executive roles as interim at this point in their careers. The only difference is the length of the contract (whether as a contract executive or as an employee). Experienced executives are more careful and cautious of the roles they step into for a number of reasons, including the impact to their brand and whether it is fun or challenging enough for them.

As a result, we are seeing a trend for executives to work with a company initially on a project or temporary basis. In our experience, about half of the time, at the start of the engagement, there is no expectation by the executive or the company of the executive transitioning to a full-time employee. In the other cases, the company is in the process of searching for a more permanent placement for the position, and they bring an interim executive in during this process and look at them as a possible fit for the full-time employee role.

For highly sought-after executives, the concept of working with the company on an interim basis first is very appealing. They are picky about what they want to do next, regardless of economic conditions. The idea of being able to try out the position and the company is attractive and advantageous. Companies see this as very appealing as well. We have received multiple comments from companies about the caliber of executive they were able to get on an interim basis versus what they have been interviewing through other sources. After working on an interim basis, the executive and company may realize there is a good longer-term fit. That's a win-win for everyone.

The pros and cons can be heavily debated for both the executive and the company. We have seen this applied to a number of situations, and the one commonality among them is the reduced risk for the parties involved. Here are a few points to consider.

The Company and the Executive End Up with More

Top-level executives are going to be just as careful to select the right organizations to work with as much as organizations will be in selecting them. At this point in their careers, their brands are highly valued, and their success and the organizations they are associated with contribute to that. Stepping in on a shorter-term basis initially gives executives a better idea of the organizations they are signing on with and how they can impact them.

Along those same lines, we often see organizations end up with higher caliber executives in Project-to-Perm arrangements than their original compensation package would have permitted. After spending some time getting to know the company, the people, and what it would take to achieve success, executives are more willing to work within the financial constraints of the organization. Since they now have hands-on experience with the opportunity, additional compensation elements, such as success bonuses, can also be more thoroughly discussed.

Goals and Deliverables Rather Than a Job Description

Rather than starting with a job description, the executive is starting with a Statement of Work (SOW) compiled by both the executive and the company. This document details what the goals are, how they will be accomplished, and the timelines in which they will get them done. This helps focus everyone at the beginning on accomplishments and results rather than a job description.

Alignment and Support

One of the most frustrating challenges for an executive is getting support from the leadership of the organization.

This is often caused by misalignment. When we talk with executives about their backgrounds, it is not uncommon to hear that they have left prior roles due to misalignment; the owner wanted to take the company in one direction, and the executive thought it should go in another. Working with the company initially as an outside contractor can provide some perspective and insight into how these decisions are made and how willing the leadership team may be to support what it will take to get to the next level.

We have seen some incredible matches as a result of an executive working at a company initially as an interim executive. Adam is one great example. Adam is a very seasoned operations executive with decades of experience in warehouse and distribution. He took an interim executive role as vice president of logistics overseeing a single facility for a multi-billion dollar distribution company. It was not a longer-term role he was interested in, though. For starters, the company was three hours away from him, and he still had one child in high school. Moving his daughter was not an option. Secondly, he didn't have much interest leading a single facility for an extended period of time. He wanted more of a challenge, and the value he could bring to one facility didn't justify the salary he would need to commit to a full-time role. After a few months in the role, the company realized the extent of Adam's talent and value to the company. Adam also got to know the leadership team and enjoyed working with them. The company ended up creating a new position, expanding the role to vice president of operations over all of the company's facilities internationally. The new role resolved the salary gap issue, and the company was amenable to Adam commuting for the next two years. Neither Adam nor the company would have considered this a possibility when the engagement began, but were both very pleased it ended up there.

There are a number of options for transitioning in and out of being an independent executive. The rest of this book will focus solely on how executives can build a successful independent executive business, whether they are looking to create an alternative career option, create a lifestyle business, or find the next challenge and help companies over the next hurdle.

Pulling It All Together

Independent executives have a variety of backgrounds and experiences that can lead to this career choice. Often, you can more successfully build an independent executive business by paying attention to what is around you and listening than by careful planning, determination, and having an illustrious previous corporate executive career. Countless experiences, opportunities, and connections can be leveraged to create a career that fits what you want to do next in life. Regardless of your background, the possible pathways for a successful independent executive career are endless.

— CASE IN POINT —

Never Speechless

Jayne Latz is CEO of Corporate Speech Solutions (CSS), serving both individuals and groups in Fortune 500 companies. As a licensed speech-language pathologist, speech trainer, and coach with twenty-five-plus years of experience, Latz launched CSS, customizing speech improvement and accent-reduction training programs to suit individuals and groups for both business and personal success.

Jayne relates her story:

"There are three people who shaped or helped shape me into the person I am today: my mother, my father, and my husband. I was a shy girl and did not speak until I was three years old. Family friends worried about me, but my mother never did. She said, 'Jayne will speak when she is ready,' and I did.

One day, when I was a teenager, my mother came home from work and excitedly said, 'I met the most interesting woman at work today. She is a speech-language pathologist.' In those days, the early 1970s, this was not a well-known career. I had never heard of it. My mother had never heard of it either. In fact, most people were not familiar with the field of speech-language pathology.

By the time I went to college, I was one of the few college freshmen who was laser-focused and knew exactly which path to pursue. I completed college and went on to get my master's degree. For the next twenty years, I worked in the medical field, helping stroke patients and the elderly to recover their voices.

My father was an inspiration because he was an entrepreneur. He owned a retail furniture store and served as a role model for being my own boss. There was always something in the back of my mind telling me to create my own business. One day, while attending a professional conference for the American Speech Language and Hearing Association (ASHA), I met a group of colleagues who were involved in a small niche in our field called Corporate Speech-Language Pathology. A light bulb went off at that moment. I was so excited. This was the perfect path for me to pursue—the blending of my background as a speech-language pathologist combined with working in the business world. The goal would be to provide training to business professionals who would benefit from speaking with greater clarity and confidence while climbing up the corporate ladder.

When I returned home from the conference, I began the mental design of my new company while still working in my traditional position in the medical environment. My husband and I began to brainstorm on the name and eventually the logo for this new venture.

Corporate Speech Solutions, LLC was born, and since that time our company has helped hundreds of corporate professionals overcome communication issues that were holding back their careers. It is my goal to share the knowledge I have acquired over the past ten years in order to help you rise up the corporate ladder."

CHAPTER 2

Building Your Independent Executive Business of One

Top Characteristics of Successful Independent Executives

We understand that most independent executives are at the top of their field. They are the best at what they do and can solve most CEOs' problems. So why isn't anyone signing on the dotted line or referring more?

By far, doing one's own business development and sales is the most challenging part of being an independent executive. We often hear, "It is so much easier to sell someone or something else than myself." One would think that, because nobody knows an executive better than him- or herself, he or she would be the best person for the task.

So why are some executives really good at it while others struggle year after year?

Independent executives don't become successful without having extensive knowledge and years of experience. However, there are some who go on to be more successful at securing opportunities than others. We have seen this more influenced by traits and characteristics than work history and methodology. Not all are needed at all times, and fortunately, most can be learned if they currently don't sit on top of your "strengths" list. As obvious as most are, there is a fine line between executives who can check them off on a list versus those who leverage them for success.

Honesty

Honesty goes well beyond the obvious "do not lie" principle. Being honest with clients and oneself can have a ripple effect in many areas. First, executives should be honest with what type of work they want to do and what they are really good at. Find the passion and don't lose sight of it.

While it is true that clients are attracted to those with impressive credentials, that doesn't mean an executive should lie or embellish accomplishments. Exaggerating work experiences and skills might land a client but will put the executive in a position they won't be qualified to deal with or take more time while they learn, causing issues for the client and damaging the executive's reputation in the process. If executives are honest about their capabilities, they'll find the clients best suited for them.

Next, an executive should not lose sight of why he or she was brought in by the client. Fear of losing a client due to telling them something the client doesn't want to hear rarely ends well. We have seen executives not be upfront with their clients about what they see because it could cut an engagement short or upset them. When working with clients, they and their company come first, so tell them the reality and not just what they want to hear. Given the nature of the situations executives are brought in to address, leaving out key pieces of information or not speaking up can be just as harmful as a flat-out lie.

Bob was working with a company situation that involved internal conflicts with the investor group, the board, and the CEO. The company was losing millions of dollars, and the cause could not be agreed upon. The investor group was looking at selling the company, but the rest of the stakeholders felt otherwise. Bob was brought in as an interim CFO to provide due diligence on the situation and his expert opinion on what should be done. Bob was retained and given SOW direction by the investor group. Within a few days of starting on the engagement, the CEO started changing the SOW to nonrelated items. The items did not correspond to Bob's original SOW created by the investor group; neither did they relate to his expertise. It was not difficult to realize there was no chance of a successful outcome in this situation. Rather than immediately contacting the investor group or bringing the situation up at the next board meeting, Bob instead chose to preserve his relationship with the CEO and the longevity of his engagement. In the end, after months of working on the engagement, this information did come to light, and the engagement was immediately terminated. The blame for the spiraling situation was then placed on Bob, and the individual who had referred him was left to do damage control. Bob never heard back from anyone in the investor group, the leadership, the board, nor the referral partner again.

Conversely, Craig was working with a similar situation in which he was brought in by a Private Equity (PE) firm for due diligence. Craig had specific industry expertise, and the PE firm wanted some outside perspective. The firm gave Craig no indication about their current position with the potential acquisition in order not to influence his findings and opinion. Craig was scheduled to spend about two weeks at the company. After four hours, Craig contacted the PE firm and, in one sentence, summed it all up: "This is not a good investment; don't do it." Craig went down the list and confirmed each item the PE firm had suspected but did not feel they had sufficient industry background to substantiate. Craig's engagement was concluded at that point, along with a lasting positive impression, and received a number of ongoing assessment requests from the firm.

Communication Skills

Good verbal and written communication skills are useful in a variety of situations. It starts with communicating what executives do best, how they do it and the impact they can have for clients. It continues when they are initially meeting with clients, the ability to quickly understand their needs, and effectively communicate their thoughts and input. It then becomes more critical than ever as they work with clients and need to convey everything from progress to problems. As we saw in the prior examples of Bob and Craig, lack of communication can lead to or help avoid critical situations. Open and succinct communication can make the difference in getting referrals—or not.

Expert Knowledge

One of the main reasons executives are approached by clients is for their expertise, which the client expects to be significantly better than that possessed by anyone internally. Because of time constraints, the client looks to the executive for help with troubleshooting problems they have no time to learn about. The executive's knowledge should be broad enough to know what questions to ask, where to research for solutions, and when to involve other executives or experts. If an executive reaches a point at which he or she is stuck and doesn't feel like the best person to solve the issue, the executive can use contacts within his or her network to reach out to for help and advice, or refer them in to the client as the expert for that particular issue.

We were contacted by an executive who worked with a group of experts within the consumer goods industry. The group was presenting to a client who wanted to automate his plant. The group had an extensive amount of experience within this industry, including operations and technology backgrounds, having done this many times before. However, they did not have specific experience on some of the automated machinery the client was looking to implement. The group had done quite a bit of research and had enough combined knowledge that they certainly could have figured it out. Instead, they searched out someone who had the specific engineering background needed and brought him in on the engagement. One of the core values they offer clients is that they are all seasoned at what they do and there is no learning on the job.

An executive's knowledge should also be current. He or she can stay updated through magazines, training, conferences, and networking with other professionals in the industry. Executives should know their expertise and their sweet spot rather than try to be all things to their client. Every penny the client spends should be invested in the best person to do the job. Additional classes, seminars, and certifications can be useful to deepen an executive's level of expertise and keep current on a range of topics that are important to clients.

Reputation

An executive's reputation is one of the most important pieces to building a successful business and can be easily harmed in a number of ways, from interactions with clients, referral network, and/or other executives. Executives should take care to maintain their reputations above everything else because once damaged, these are hard to fix. This is why so many executives carefully vet people they work with and clients they take on. According to the 2015 The Independent Executive survey[6], almost 63 percent of all new business comes from referrals. Having any of your referral network question your integrity or abilities can have a lasting impact.

This starts with being realistic with what an executive can do for a client, what the client needs, and what is best for the client, rather than focusing on how much money the executive can make. If the executive isn't the best match for what is needed, he or she needs to refer the client to someone

---

[6] https://ceriusexecutives.com/interim-executive-confidential-independent-executive-4/

who can do a better job for them. Next, it's important to be clear about what is realistic and plausible. Yes, most clients' visions are possible, but be realistic with them about what it will take to get there. Finally, be respectful of fellow independent executives. We have seen executives so focused on getting their next engagement that they lose sight of the value of their referral relationships and are willing to undercut, circumvent, or promise beyond what is possible to get work.

Analytical Skills

Clients don't entirely trust executives who seemingly create solutions out of thin air. Even if an executive is confident in his or her problem-solving abilities, the executive should consider spending time on planning and investigation. The ability to solve problems based on solid facts and research helps to make sound decisions.

Experience weighs in heavily as well, and if you have lots of it, it can be a great asset in making business decisions for both you and your client. James struggled with this. Though he certainly had background and knowledge that could be applied to the clients he was meeting with, he wasn't taking the time to learn about each specific situation before jumping to any conclusions. One of his clients was immediately turned off no more than five minutes into the meeting. As they were touring their site, James quickly started commenting on the issues he saw and how he would fix them, with no other information yet from the owner. The owner was done with the meeting about ten minutes into it.

Gather all of the information first and listen before trying to solve a client's problem.

Sociability

If the executive is a person who comes into the office with no intent of befriending anyone—just work, get paid, and go home—then this may not be the career path for them. It requires people skills. Having some social skills, e.g., humor and confidence, will make people want to listen and engage. The ability to put clients at ease helps an executive gain the confidence to be able to draw out needed information. This helps the executive to better understand the company, culture, and issues.

If an executive has no interest in learning about other people (both professionally and personally), again, this may not be the best career path for them. People want to work with people they like. Starting a networking conversation off with, "So what do you do?" or, "Do you have any clients who could use my skill sets?" are not the best icebreakers. Take a little time to get to know the individual before determining whether it makes sense to connect again for a further conversation.

Professionalism

It's very important for executives to maintain a high level of professionalism. This should be consistent, from their profile picture to the rest of their online digital footprint to the simplest interactions with clients, such as e-mails. Be cautious of using pictures with the family dog or kids as a LinkedIn picture, and watch what is posted on a Facebook page set to public view. More times than not, we all have at least a few professional acquaintances on Facebook or Twitter; if executives want to feel free to post what they want, they should consider cleaning up their Friends list first. When e-mailing or texting, emoji or abbreviations should be used with care. It's better to spell it out so the message is clear and concise as a professional.

Keeping Ego in Check

An accomplished executive will always have some ego, but it should be balanced with some humility. Executives may be the best at what they do, but a big ego will get in the way more times than not. We aren't talking about walking around with one's chest puffed up and incessantly bragging about oneself. It is often the little things that can easily turn clients off. It can be as simple as telling clients they are doing something wrong, correcting them to show the executive knows what he or she is talking about, or doing all of the talking to keep the focus on the executive rather than the clients. An executive should be cautious that his or her words and actions don't come across as too boastful to others. Remember, the executive is there to make clients and their teams the heroes, not themselves.

Starting with the Right Foundation: The Independent Executive's Tool Kit

These tools range greatly, from those that are used to build and run an independent executive business to those used to help client's businesses. They can help reinforce the executive's brand, establish a value proposition, differentiate the executive from the 3,048 other executives who do something similar, and often simply make life easier. From productivity tools to sales and marketing to client engagement, an independent executive's toolkit can be the difference between a successful business and a struggling business.

So, let's say an executive is a former CFO and will now be working independently as an interim executive or management consultant. He or she no longer has an organization (regardless of how big or small) providing the tools needed to do the job and serve the customer. The executive also no longer has coworkers to rely on for information and tools. As an independent executive, what tools should executives have at their disposal during the transition to help communicate what they do best and serve their clients?

We have seen some fairly extensive toolkits over the years. Some executives have even taken the unique tools they have come up with and transitioned them into a broader business centered around them. Others have transitioned their tools into a technology platform and created a technology-enabled business startup from it. We'll discuss how executives can leverage their toolbox into an ongoing revenue stream in chapter 9. What is simply "helpful" now could become your number one source of revenue a few years from now.

There are more resources out there than one can imagine for piecing together what is most useful to each executive.

Executives should beware of getting so lost putting everything together that they lose sight of building their business and serving their clients. The tools should support, not interfere, detract, or deter. Something being "cool," or developing it because "everyone else is" falls into these categories. Keep the focus on your business and the client's business, and the question of whether it is needed or not.

Pulling It All Together

Most executives we meet possess many, if not all, of the characteristics described in this chapter. It is how they are applied and leveraged that starts to mark the difference between one executive to the next.

Because the most common struggle across the board is getting leads and closing business, we are focusing the rest of the book on three key areas: marketing, business development, and sales. Many will see marketing and business development as interchangeable in an independent executive business (especially a business of one), which is a reason so many continue to struggle while others experience success.

There is No One-Size-Fits-All: Use Multiple Marketing and Business Development Strategies

Not all successful independent executives take the same path or use the same playbook. They may end up with the same outcome of more clients, but build their business in a variety of different ways. What they all have in common is that they play to their strengths. If they love meeting new people, talking, and chatting, then networking and events are great resources. If they love to write and keep up on current news, leveraging social media and a strong online footprint may be more comfortable and productive. The important thing is to be sure not to rely entirely on areas of comfort, but instead to make progress on all marketing and business development fronts.

As in most situations, independent executives should never rely on just one source for all of their business-building. We'll go into each in more detail in chapters 3 and 4. For starters, here's a brief overview of the top marketing and business development channels we have seen independent executives use.

- **Social Media**—This is a great place to reinforce your brand and your expertise. What is the one thing you want to be known for? That should be the theme throughout your communications, postings, tweets, blogs, etc.

- **Intermediaries and Online Marketplaces**—It's always great when someone else can do most of your marketing and business development for you. Both of these are growing areas and are worth the time investment.

- **Networking**—It is wonderful when you can show up to a networking function and meet someone who needs your help, but since that doesn't happen very often, go to networking events with targets in mind. Is someone you know attending or one of the speakers? Do your research on them so when you do meet them at these events, you can carry on a conversation that will pique their interest in you.

- **Referrals**—These are past employers, past clients, networking contacts, social media contacts, etc. The number one thing we can say is, "Keep in Touch Regularly!"

For the independent executive, marketing is determining what you will market, and business development is taking it to market. We see too many executives skip marketing altogether and focus solely on business development, then wonder why they have only received one referral in three months, despite the number of networking events, e-mails, and meetings they have had. It must start with marketing. Get the marketing right, and the rest of the puzzle will come together much easier than you can imagine.

SECTION II

How to Build a Successful Business of One

CHAPTER 3

Brand Yourself

Your Executive Brand + Your Expertise + Perceived Perception = Your Differentiation and Value to a Client

Consider marketing as the product development area of your business. In the case of independent executives, the product is their brand. Without a brand, you are likely seen as the proverbial "consultant who decided to hang a shingle out and see what happened." This is becoming so critical that we are seeing a growing sector of consultants serving the independent executive industry starting to gain momentum. Branding and marketing experts have realized there is an untapped marketplace for independent executives. Essentially, consultants are providing their expertise as a product to the independent executive. This is being driven by the growth of the segment and the extent of the channels and tools for taking your brand to market. We expect to see this trend continue to expand as executives build and grow their businesses around what they do best. Where there's a growing business, there's a need for services and support.

The importance of building an executive brand has been on the rise in the past decade. With the advancement of technology and growth of social media, we believe that today more than ever before, it is important to create the right brand to convey the impact you can create for your clients. One of the biggest challenges for executives with long careers is communicating what they can do for potential clients. Those wanting to market themselves independently have to create a personal brand to get the right message across. Not everyone an executive comes in contact with can spend a few hours discussing backgrounds, resumes, CVs, bios, and understanding what they have done, what they do best, and how they can help companies. Instead, they must rely on small snippets of information and messaging to convey the key points.

What Is an Executive Brand?

An executive brand is what people say about you when you are not in the room and is defined by the executive. Although the latter is shaped by experiences associated with the corporate brand, the two are distinctly separate entities. Essentially, the top ten results on Google when you search for the executive highlight the executive brand. Creating an executive brand takes time and effort, but can become one of the most useful and effective tools in building your business.

Creating an Executive Brand

Start with your past. Get your entire history on paper so you can easily pull what you need. Jot down all of your work experiences, skills, and achievements in a single document. Most of this information you can pull from your CV, resume, portfolio, and online profiles. Reflect on your past work history and make a list of the results you have delivered and can deliver to future clients. By determining what value you bring to a client, you can better market and sell yourself.

We get the opportunity to have background discussions regularly with executives. Without fail, it ends up as a branding discussion. One inevitably leads to the other. We can't talk through an executive's background without ending up at, "How do you impact companies?" It all starts with the background. It is surprising what some tend to forget, especially if they have been independent for some time.

Here's one example of a common discussion we have.

Frank had been working diligently for months on his marketing. He hired someone to help him build a website, assist with his messaging, and was working with a few other executives on business referrals. Frank was giving an overview of what he did and how he helped companies. He was very excited about the headline on his home page, "Business Transformation." He then went on to talk about all the various ways he transforms businesses through process re-engineering, culture change, etc. About fifty minutes into the phone call, he shared a story about how he and a business partner had purchased a company out of bankruptcy and two years later, had grown it more than 800 percent and was in the black with $220 million in profit. Kristen's response was, "Why are you waiting until this point in the conversation to mention this? Make this your lead-in!" It had been about eight years ago and he had somewhat forgotten about it. Get your history down on paper and start from there.

"I Can Do That" Versus "I Am an Expert"

Being brought in as an independent executive can be very different from being hired as a full-time executive. Rather than a broad job description, there is usually a defined scope of work, set of deliverables, established timelines, and a specified end. You are brought in to either accomplish a goal, fix a challenging situation, or step into a specific role for a short period of time. All of these require a high level of expertise. Be cautious about extrapolating some experience to expertise. Having been a president of a company with responsibility for sales does not in itself qualify an executive to be an interim vice president of sales. The same applies to a CFO with HR reporting to him or her in the last two jobs. This alone does not qualify the executive as an expert in HR. As an interim, being a quick learner or having some foundation in an area is not enough. Be clear about what you are an expert at, and have multiple examples with which you can convey what you have accomplished before.

Expertise and skills sets are increasingly becoming one of the top criteria filters online for a reason. As you look through online marketplaces of all types (we cover this more later in the chapter), you will see "skill sets" or "expertise" as one of the top filters in any search. Companies looking to bring in outsourced talent need something specific to be accomplished. They want someone who is an expert in that area. Our rule of thumb is, if you can write a credible article or give a presentation to your peers on the topic, you can count yourself an expert, with the caveat that you have also done it repeatedly in practice as well. This should be consistent with your resume, your profiles, and your content. The more we have seen executives brand themselves with their expertise, the more successful they have been with referrals and opportunities. It is one of the best ways to differentiate yourself. Be cautious of trying to be the person who can do any and all engagements because you are a great "learner." Companies do not bring in an independent executive to learn on the job. They bring them in so the company can learn from them. We will expand on this in more detail throughout this book.

Don't Assume You Know Yourself Best

It is amazing how two people can be talking about the same thing, but describing it two different ways. Each person has his or her own perspective and will apply what you do to that perspective and their experiences. If you are basing the messaging of your brand solely on what you come up with on your own, you may be off the mark, given the importance of your referral network and potential client's perspective. You want to describe what you can do for companies in the same or similar words that your potential clients would describe it. The best source to figure this out is past clients or colleagues with whom you have worked. The words you use and the point you are getting across should be phrased from their perspective. Be careful of focusing too much on what you want, and keep in mind what your potential clients need. James is an example of this disconnect.

James is a great all-around executive. He has a good background in both operations and technology. In his conversations with referral partners and potential clients, he talks about how he provides operational efficiencies and improved processes through technology. In his mind, this is the value he brings his clients. However, if you talk to one of his clients, the conversation would be more centered around how James stepped into an enterprise resource planning (ERP) implementation process that was going off-track. James was able to connect the needs of the business and all of its stakeholders with much-needed technology to help them do their jobs better. James helped join the operations of the business with the technology that was there to support its needs rather than letting the technology dictate how the company should function. James was speaking his language— what he did to help—rather than the client's language—the problem he solved.

It is helpful to step back and stop thinking like an executive or a consultant and think more like a client. Put yourself in their shoes.

Narrowing Down Your Expertise

When bringing in an independent executive, a client wants the best person to solve their problem. Part of building trust is showing how you are the right person to help them. They need some type of evidence beyond you telling them you are the right person. The more you can focus and relate your expertise and your background to their situation, the higher their comfort level will be that you are the right person. Part of that is drawing the connection for them. Take your history and package it up in a way that a client will start to see the picture and make the connection between what you have done and what you can do for them, often before even meeting you. This is where things can certainly get challenging. How do you take twenty to thirty-plus years of work experience and all that you've done and narrow that expertise down into either a summary or overview, highlighting only the most important pieces?

Since you don't have the opportunity to initially be in front of and have a direct conversation with all of your future clients, you must rely on someone else or your digital presence to convey your brand and your story. To accomplish this:

1. Your referral peers must completely understand what you do and always keep you top-of-mind when they are speaking to a client who has a particular need you can fill.

2. Your digital presence must quickly convey and relate how you can help clients—using the type of language they would use.

This is extremely difficult for most executives. Since most have either been hands-on or managed every part of the organization, narrowing it down to a few areas of expertise is not easy. This is further complicated by résumés that list job titles and not individual expertise.

A Common Myth

The most common myth we hear is that if you focus

on just one area, you may miss an opportunity or an engagement because you can help clients in a variety of areas. The reality is that you are more likely missing out on more opportunities because your peers don't know when and how to recommend you. This is caused by casting too wide a net. If there's an opportunity to refer someone, people are more likely to refer someone who is a specialist in the company's need and situation, rather than someone who simply says "I help grow companies."

As an executive, you do have a diverse skill set. You had to have it to get to the level where you are today. For example, let's say you're a marketing executive who eventually ran your own company, so now you know sales, marketing, and operations, and you've done various business deals that have given you lots of experience in contract law. Are you an expert in all of these areas? Likely not. So how do you pick just the ones in which you really are an expert?

Ask yourself this question: "Right now, if I had to get up on stage in front of fifty of my peers, what subject or situation could I speak to as an expert?" This includes being able to cite multiple case studies or examples. To make your point and relate it to real situations, you would relate a story about what had been happening, what you did to intervene, and why it was so successful. If you can't stand up in front of your peers with confidence that you are an expert, teaching them something that they either don't know or are being offered a new perspective on, be cautious of presenting yourself as an expert on the topic. Another way of looking at it: If you were to ask ten former supervisors, peers, or clients to rate you on a scale from one to five, with five being the highest, would they rate you a four or five in the area?

We see the term "expert" used broadly at the executive level. Here's a scenario to help put that into perspective. You are an owner of a small marketing services company. Would fifty sales executives pay to hear you talk about sales and business development? Probably not. If, however, your audience is other small marketing service company owners and you are talking about how you grew your company from $250k to $5 million in two years, you likely would draw a paying audience. Narrow your focus down to what situations you can be dropped into and be the expert.

Your Sweet Spot

Your sweet spot is a combination of what you are great at and what you love to do. It is about tapping into your authentic self. Your authenticity about who you serve, why you serve them, and how you serve them will help those things you are struggling to communicate come more naturally.

Start by identifying what you do best and what you enjoy most, both at the same time. This zone is where you are unstoppable. If you're the go-to person for specific types of situations, people will want to know that, because this is where you are more likely to succeed and perform best. Compare that to "what a company is willing to pay for and what they see value in," and you are headed in the right direction.

So how do you find your sweet spot? Try this little exercise.

List at least ten accomplishments that you have been proud of in your past, and more importantly, ones which you thoroughly enjoyed the process. This list isn't for your resume, but rather for your introspection, so stay honest and don't focus on thinking it through too much.

When we are in a sweet spot, typically our competence is subconscious. Most of the time, we are not even aware of the different steps we take in performing activities we're a master in. Think about your accomplishments and note what steps you took to achieve them. Itemize all the steps under each one of your accomplishments and you'll likely notice a common denominator.

If you aren't able to answer the single question, "What is your brand," this may be a good place to start. This can help serve as the starting point as you determine your expertise and your brand.

As difficult as it may be initially, bottom line—brand yourself!

Communicating Your Brand

As an independent executive, it is now all about you and your brand. Manage your brand the same way a Fortune 500 company would manage theirs. What do you want to be known for? Is your information and the look and feel across your online and offline footprint consistent? If two people meet and find out they both know you, would they both say essentially the same thing about you? What is that? What they say should be consistent with the brand you are intending to convey.

Just telling people your accomplishments may not be enough. Package your career sweet spot into a memorable example that explains to the referral partner how you work and can help clients. If you leave the guesswork up to someone else regarding how your expertise can be applied, it rarely turns out well. Make it easy and tell them.

Look at all of the time you spend networking. Consider your elevator pitch. Are you focusing on you or on how you help your clients? Tell people what you do best and the impact it has (the use of numbers is great), relating it to your career sweet spot.

James can simply tell people that he provides operation efficiencies and process improvements to companies. The problem is, most clients do not say, "I need someone to help me with operational efficiencies." If we use the example of the client James helped with the ERP system, that client is going to discuss the headaches of how the IT department was not listening to anyone else in the company and was trying to dictate how they would operate the business. James needs to convey what he did with examples such as, "I helped a company implement a multi-million-dollar ERP system resulting in an annualized savings of 5 percent to their bottom line by focusing on how the technology could enable the needs of the business rather than the other way around." The next time anyone to whom James has told this story hears someone complain about IT not supporting the business, they will think of James. They may not even mention ERP, but the fact that he helped add 5 percent to the bottom line through a successful integration of technology, keeping in mind the business's needs first, will be far more compelling than him talking about "operational efficiencies."

Remember back to the Frank example at the beginning of the chapter. When a company is in trouble, they generally aren't thinking, "I need a business transformation specialist." What they are thinking is, "I need help figuring out where the issues are in my company and fixing them." Or more specifically, "I am losing money on the plant floor daily and I can't figure out where and how to fix it."

Show Me the Numbers

You are no longer VP of sales or COO for XYZ Corp. You are a problem-solver. You no longer have a list of your role and responsibilities; you have a list of ways you have helped clients. In your conversations, be clear on "here's the type of issues I solve." Most companies don't say, "I'm looking for a part-time VP of sales" or "I need someone with sales management expertise." Instead, they say, "I have a sales problem," but leave out that they are looking for someone to solve it. To help with that, make yourself impressive and memorable. Nothing does that better than numbers. You want someone to be able to meet you today and remember the types of problems you have solved and what kind of impact you have made weeks or months later.

The more easily referral sources can remember this information, the more they will remember you when the next CEO is discussing his sales issues. They will remember your story about a similar sales situation and the results you got for the client. Kristen's conversation with Frank about the bankruptcy turnaround situation was over a year ago. She still clearly remembers his example.

As an interim executive, your background is no longer about the responsibilities you had at the last five companies. That information should be replaced with key accomplishments and results at your last five clients (or positions if you recently transitioned). Selling yourself as an independent executive is about selling results and outcomes. When a company needs an independent executive, they don't necessarily need a person who has X, Y, Z experience; they need someone who can accomplish and deliver successful outcomes. We review hundreds of resumes and profiles each week; this is the number one thing missing and conversely, the number one request from clients. "What have they accomplished in the past, and what types of results have they delivered for other companies?" Given the tremendous amount of experience an executive has, clients looking to bring on an interim executive or advisor are not looking for whether he or she has had Profit and Loss (PNL) responsibility. That is assumed at this point. What impact the executive has had on PNL is what they are more concerned about. Leave the job responsibilities on your CV and focus on the results you have accomplished in your last couple of positions or projects.

Don't be modest, and don't be stingy with numbers. As much as clients do appreciate that you "increased morale," they are far more impressed that you "reduced turnover by 20 percent." How much did you help grow sales by or improve EBITDA? A client is looking for specific results. Rather than, "I increased sales," say, "Sales increased by 32 percent year-over-year while the operating budget was reduced by 5 percent." Rather than saying, "I am a versatile executive with more than twenty years of experience in the C-suite who can help companies maximize value and increase returns," consider using a specific example that exemplifies what you can do for a company: "I have more than twenty years of experience working with startup companies in the energy industry. The last three firms I worked with each exited within five years for multiples of eight to ten times EBIDTA." Another common description we hear is, "I work with small growing companies and help them get past the curve where their sales have outgrown the talent of their team." We recommend adding at least one specific example like, "I helped the last company I worked with grow from $10 million to a run rate of $18 million and increase their net profit by 50 percent in the nine months I was there."

Here's a great example of how one executive chose to niche her business within a single industry and built her brand by the numbers.

— CASE IN POINT —

Dentists by The Numbers

Penny Reed has worked with dentists and spoken to dental groups for more than twenty-five years. Her articles have been published in numerous trade publications including *Dental Economics*, *Dentistry Today*, and *Inside Dentistry*. She was selected by *Dentistry Today* as one of their prestigious Leaders in Dental Consulting.

Here are Reed's top five ways to grow a dental business:

1. Increase New Patients by 10 Percent

A thriving dental practice should have a minimum of twenty-five new patients (comprehensive exams) per full-time doctor per month. If the value of a new patient is $2,000, and a dentist increases productivity by 10 percent, or three new patients per month, a dentist's revenue would increase like this: three additional new patients per month at $2,000 per new patient = $6,000 per month in additional production.

2. Increase Active Patients by 10 Percent

Increasing the active number of patients means not only adding new patients, but also ensuring the total active patient base is growing and not shrinking. In a practice with 2,000 active patients (an active patient is a patient who has been in to the office in the last 24 months), then an increase in 10 percent would translate to increased annual revenues of $40,000.

3. Increase Hygiene Membership by 10 Percent

Another growth factor is to have more patients in the practice see the hygienist regularly to increase revenue and overall dental health. For a dental practice with 2,000 active patients, that can translate to increased annual revenues of $59,600 (and many more healthy sets of teeth).

4. Increase Case Acceptance by 5 Percent

If the patient visit value is $200, and dental practices increase it by 5 percent, the dental office raises the value by $10 per patient visit for a total of $210 per patient visit average. That change produces an additional income of $10 per visit, at 6,144 visits per year. The monthly increase would be $5,120, with a $61,440 annual increase.

5. Maximize Efficiency of Provider Time by 10 Percent

In an eight-hour day, this would mean streamlining systems to allow almost an additional hour of primary provider time (doctor or hygienist). A dental office should focus on freeing up thirty minutes (three ten-minute units) of primary time in operative and the same amount for hygiene. That could add up to $75,000 more revenue in a year.

"Dentists need to see the potential," says Reed. "For an office that already has annual revenues of $1.2 million, these changes can result in a potential growth opportunity of more than $296,000."

Instead of focusing on aspects of the dental economy they cannot control, Penny directs a dentist's focus to the five areas that drive growth in their business, which fall into three broader categories: marketing, engagement, and organization.

Keep Your Information Consistent

Don't tell a networking group you are looking for your next COO role when the last four positions on your online profile were all CFO positions. It's understandable to want to look for entirely different roles, but companies want executives who bring years of relevant experience to the table. So, make your information consistent with your history and what you want. It is also confusing and frustrating when someone you meet finds nothing from your conversation reflected on your LinkedIn profile. Regardless of where you display your information, whether on LinkedIn, Twitter, Facebook, Instagram, etc., it needs to be consistent across the board and highlight your expertise.

Build the Bridge Between Your Past and Client Needs

Don't just list facts and data; list accomplishments, impact, and results. The challenge of listing the roles you have held and what you were responsible for is that you are asking a potential client to make the connection. As we've mentioned, when a potential client needs to figure out what you've done, what the problems were, what you did to solve them, and then draw the parallel to their situation, you are asking them to do too much work. Make it easy for them. Rather than saying "I establish processes and procedures," share stories about another company that was in a similar situation, what you put in place, and what types of results they achieved. What problems did the processes and procedures help solve? What was the result of implementing them? As a CEO, I likely do not know at this point that I need to put processes and procedures in place. What I do know is that I have problems, and if I read about a company you worked with that had the same problems and how you solved them, I can quickly and easily relate to them.

Never Underestimate the Power of a Good Story

Never underestimate what a good story can do to communicate your brand and how you serve others. Here's an example of how one executive built his business with a story.

— CASE IN POINT —

To the Arctic and Back

Mike Pierce's flagship program, *Leading at 90 Below Zero*, connects principles of Antarctic expedition history and his own adventures there to the real world of finding, engaging, and keeping great people in today's business world.

In January 2006, I became one of nine people to run a marathon (26.2 miles) on the Antarctic continent. About a year later, I returned to the Antarctic to become the first American to complete the Antarctica Ultramarathon, a grueling 100 kilometers (62.1 miles). The attraction to run in Antarctica had very little to do with sports or cold weather; rather, it was an opportunity to follow in the footsteps of my polar heroes who were the first to have conquered Antarctica, Robert Falcon Scott and Roald Amundsen.

Since then, I have completed many other winter marathons in the coldest and harshest climates on earth.

After graduating from college, I soon went to work in sales. My first real struggle in sales was when I got into the insurance business. I never loved it. I liked it, I tolerated it, I knew it could make money, and I put a roof over my head for a few years doing it, but I never loved it.

Because in those days, at that insurance company, you got a license and then the company put you on the street and said "good luck." They wanted you to sink or swim. At the outset, I sank. I remember my first day in the business. I was taken into an interior office with no windows, and it was about the size of a large closet. My manager assigned me one of the two desks in the room and said, "Here's your desk; good luck. Come and see us when you have a check and a contract. And by the way, you owe us $52, because we already turned your phone on."

What I soon discovered is that the biggest and most expensive problem a company has with respect to people isn't hiring them, it's actually keeping them. By that, I mean making sure that their people are consistently and fully engaged in what they do every day.

During a business trip in Bakersfield, California in 2001, I happened upon a book in a Barnes & Noble called *Shackleton's Way*. I was fascinated by Ernest Shackleton's heroic tale of leading a team of twenty-seven men to be the first to cross the entire Antarctic continent on foot, some 1,800 miles. I read stories of other heroic polar expeditions. I knew that the lessons in the stories of these polar adventures were a great metaphor to teach principles of leadership and success.

My thinking was Antarctic exploration was the metaphor that would help me make the points I wanted to make. So, I threw my company's PowerPoint in the trash. I put in all the pictures from the Shackleton story. The training course I wrote for my company was a huge hit. That's when I started longing to do this for a thousand companies, not just one.

During my talks to sales leaders and sales reps about what they can learn from the Antarctic explorations, I share a number of lessons that leaders can use to help them find, engage, and keep the best-performing people. That is how I went from a frustrated insurance agent to an author and speaker who travels internationally to inspire corporate leaders and sales reps. My message is simple:

"Everybody has an Antarctica to conquer. Keep conquering."

What's your story? Now go tell it!

Get the Word Out

Get it out there— everyone you speak to should be clear on what you do best and what opportunities you are looking for. With the current business and talent environment, it is rare for anyone to not come across an open opportunity or position here and there. Companies and recruiters are looking for talent referrals more than ever. Make sure everyone you come across knows what you are looking for and when to keep you in mind. You are more likely to find your next opportunity through someone you know than through a posting.

Send e-mails; write blogs; post updates on what you are up to. It often takes three to five posts or e-mails for the receiver to not only read but also remember what you said. Use social media posts to stay current, relevant, and authentic with your network. For example, "Great client meeting today—young CEO with great insights needs me to help determine next growth strategy for his company." No need to disclose any details or the company/CEO name. Your network will enjoy seeing these and they are a lot more memorable than a single e-mail announcement.

Become a Thought Leader

A great way to establish yourself as the expert and create value for potential prospects is to publish consumable content. You likely won't be meeting all of your future clients at networking events; they could come from other sources, such as referral partners or your online presence. Information about what you do and how you address pains in the marketplace that can be easily consumed by your target audience is worthy of time and investment. Content can be in the form of articles/blogs, tweets, posts, slide shows, presentations, podcasts, videos, etc. The one thing the audience has in common is that they all consume information differently. Even if you don't see yourself as a writer, there are too many options available for this to be your stumbling block. Be careful of falling into the same trap when it comes to creating content as clients do when they don't address the issues they have.

There is rarely an interaction you have or something you accomplish that can't be turned into content. Look for ways to leverage your expertise or your engagements. Here are a few of the basics:

Case Studies

Document your engagements as you complete them. Every engagement should have some type of case study attached to it. These can be the most powerful tool in your marketing and business development efforts. Case studies showcase both your expertise and the types of results you've achieved for clients. Since much of what you will share is confidential information, keep it blind. For example, describe the company in terms of size and industry. Rather than sharing the exact dollar amount by which you increased revenues, use percentages. Include the reason the company brought you in, what you accomplished, the results of your efforts, and a testimonial from your client. Potential clients and referral partners should be able to consume the information in less than two minutes. There is likely nothing you could tell them verbally in two minutes that would have the same impact.

Articles

Articles are great because of their distribution and forwarding opportunities. An article can be on a timely news topic and your expert commentary on it, some guidelines or common mistakes companies make within your realm of expertise, or a recap of a previous engagement, telling the story from your client's perspective. The first comment we usually get when we recommend this is, "I'm not a very good writer." There are many great writers using online marketplaces whom you can hire to do the writing for you. These articles can be used on your website or blog, as postings on social media sites, for e-mail campaigns, or just for forwarding to referral sources or companies you want to stay in touch with.

Speaking Opportunities

Speaking opportunities are one of the most effective ways for your expertise to resonate with an audience of potential clients or referral sources. The audience is very targeted. They self-select based on interest in the topic and will sit and listen for forty-five to sixty minutes or more, depending on how engaging the speaker and topic are. Add this to your list when meeting with referral sources. Give them an idea of topics you have or could speak on. Start counting the number of associations and events that are hosted in your area in any given year. The opportunities are plentiful. It is up to you to make the connection between what would be of value to the audience and what information you can offer, consistent with your brand, in an interesting and engaging manner. The more speaking you do, the more likely it is that you will be remembered when an opportunity arises. When you do speak or get on a panel, don't rely on the audience searching you out and keeping your information. Provide some type of supporting material, preferably electronically, and offer it to anyone who gives you their business card. There should be a call to action (CTA) in most of your activities.

Executive Matchmaking Companies

Executive matchmaking companies have been around in many forms for decades. From executive recruiting firms to up-and-coming technology-enabled online marketplaces, there is a wide range of companies to help executives find their next "gig," whether it is a full-time role or their next interim engagement. Because this book is focused on the independent executive, we will limit information to full-service firms and the online platforms within this space. Looking back to the start of Cerius, it made a lot more sense to have the select few who were really good at marketing, business development, and sales represent the hundreds (and now thousands and tens of thousands) who are best at working directly on the engagement. In an ideal world, these select few could bring enough business to the masses that there would be no need for individual efforts in these key areas. Unfortunately, supply still by far outweighs demand, so the vast majority of independent executives are unable to solely rely on these companies.

Full-Service Firms

These are typically boutique-size or larger companies who act as a broker between the client company and executives. Though executive recruiting has been around for decades and most companies and executives are well aware of them, in the independent executive space, there are not as many, compared to their counterparts. As a result, there are fewer companies to get the word out and represent this growing population. With the growth of the independent executive segment, we expect this to change in the next few years.

With the newness within the space at this point, there isn't yet a set standard for the independent marketplace. As everyone looks to improve and understand what each side of the equation needs, here are a few things to consider when determining whether this is a good option for you and who to work with.

1. **CV/Resume/Profile.** How is your information, particularly your resume, being handled? Are you contacted prior to your resume/background being shown or discussed with any clients? Are they speaking with you first and finding out more information prior to sending it to the client? Are you one of ten candidates the company is looking at, or one of two? Though there is no way to know across the board, each firm likely has a standard or average they work with and can give you an idea. Either way, most responses to these questions are neither good nor bad, it will depend on your preferences.

2. **Communication.** Depending on whether you are paying for the service or not, the amount of contact and updates you receive will vary greatly. Get some clarity from the intermediary about what you can expect and make sure that meets your expectations

and there is enough value in it for you.

3. Fee Structure.

A. Membership/Subscription Model. You pay a monthly or annual membership fee to be listed on their site. Some provide additional services for increased level of membership or additional fees. You get the benefit of their marketing efforts, and most everything else in the process is up to you. It is solely a lead source. You do not need to be exclusive to any one site or service.

B. Revenue Share. There are no direct up-front costs to you, other than your time investment going through the initial process of signing up and any other processes that may exist. Any job you get through the company is done on a revenue-share basis. For example, if the share is 70/30 and the client is billed $1,000, you receive $700 of the $1,000. You gain the benefit of their marketing, sales, contracts, negotiations, and billing, to name a few. Most of your focus is on the initial discussions with the client, understanding what they need, translating that into an SOW, and doing the work itself.

C. Partnership. This is a combination of an up-front investment or "buy-in" and a revenue share. You gain the benefit of their brand, systems, marketing and internal referral network. You are exclusive to this brand. Regardless of where your leads originate, the revenue share will apply.

4. **Exclusivity.** You can do business under any of the online marketplaces, as there is no exclusivity required to join.

5. **Process.** Understand what their process is and set realistic expectations. These can vary greatly from company to company. Is it simply submitting your resume, or will more information be needed, requiring more of a time investment on your part? What are the steps they use to get to know you and your skill sets, and at what part of the process? For example, is all of the information they need gathered at the point of sign-up/application, is it gathered over time, or do they wait until there is a potential opportunity? Most will gather some basic information from you at the beginning with no further time investment until there is a potential opportunity.

6. **Type of Work.** Intermediaries will generally focus on types of work and types of clients. For example, is it mostly hourly, project-based, boards, or part-time/interim executive engagements? Is their client base primarily SMB, Fortune 500, nonprofits, or the private equity/investment community? They may also be focused more on individual placements, such as interim executives versus putting together teams of consultants for big projects. Take this into account

when you are considering the type of structure, environments, and arrangements you want to work in.

7. **Client Vetting.** How much information do they know about the client and can they share with you? Are most of their engagements straightforward, or do they need to spend time with the client understanding their end goal in order to help them better formulate the executive expertise they need? They should also be watching for red flags with the client and be willing to walk away from the client at any point.

As always, keep in mind you may never receive any business from any one intermediary, and it all comes from referrals. Keep your expectations realistic. One thing to remember is that intermediaries can be one source of leads, but like your other sources, these may be plentiful or may bear nothing. We would highly recommend not relying solely on these and certainly not solely on any one. You decide how much support you need in the process and how much you are willing or not willing to invest up front versus on the back end.

Online Marketplaces

Online marketplaces are on the rise and have been rapidly proliferating in the past few years. They are very similar to intermediaries, but are more technology-driven and more directly connect the company with the executive. Having an online lead source can be an easy way to give yourself visibility to more companies and projects. If you don't have a consistent source of leads, either from building it up through the years or from your days in your prior career, an online marketplace can be very advantageous.

The availability of these marketplaces does give you the option to do your due diligence. The interesting thing is that executives are being very picky about which ones they sign up for due to mixed experiences with both intermediaries and online marketplaces. Major concerns include their time investment, the sale or distribution of their information without permission, the quality and reputation of the database, and the types of clients. There is also the brand fear associated with being part of what may be perceived as a tainted database. Do your due diligence and be clear on your requirements and your intent regarding how they fit into your overall marketing strategy.

You can use the same list to evaluate online marketplaces as noted above, with some distinct differences. For example:

- Online marketplaces create more direct competition with other executives since opportunity alerts go out to many executives, so sharpen your differentiation and sales skills.

- The client vetting is more reliant on you. Since interactions are more technology-driven and not relationship-driven, the intermediary typically doesn't know much more than you do from their profile.

- Client vetting and evaluation of opportunity viability are now up to you.

- More of the sales process (understanding what the client needs, convincing the client you have the right expertise, and getting the client's signature) is now your responsibility.

Writing Independent Executive Online Profiles

As a top-level executive with an extensive career, writing an online profile or resume can be overwhelming. This increases for independent executives because of the variety and volume of engagements one has over time.

What is the right information to include in a profile? How much detail should be included? How far back in time should your resume or online profile cover? What often gets lost in multiple resumes, bios, and online profiles is what you do best and what you love to do.

The process presents the same challenge as branding. You have had a long career encompassing a variety of positions, engagements, and projects where you have had an opportunity to learn and accomplish quite a bit. In some cases, you were the jack-of-all-trades, and in others, you were singularly focused on a specific area. You are told time and time again to just put highlights on your resume and keep it to no more than (preferably) two pages. Given all of this advice, we have seen a dichotomy in the marketplace when it comes to executive resumes and profiles. Here are our thoughts on some of the key points when putting these together.

1. Should you include your entire work history?

As a rule of thumb, if your history covers more

than twenty years, it is acceptable to cover just the past twenty. For those who have been working independently, include information about the types of projects you have done. The reader should get an idea of what types of companies you have worked with (size, industry, ownership) and what you accomplished for them. If these are too numerous to list, have a full list available when needed and choose from those that best support your brand.

2. **Help tell the story.** As difficult as it may be, help the reader by telling a story with your information. The reader should have a clear idea of what types of companies or situations you work with, how you help, and the impact you make. Consider the "Work Experience" section as a list of short stories to support this.

3. **List accomplishments and results for the companies due to your efforts.** Rather than reiterating the job description, key in on what was accomplished during your tenure and how the company benefited from it.

4. **What kind of experience should you include?** When completing information about roles you can step into or skill sets you have, only select those in which you have hands-on experience, not just supervisory or leadership experience. Having been responsible for HR as a CFO does not necessarily equate to HR Executive as one of your "Functional Roles."

Companies want executives who can show they have solved specific problems or done the job a number of times and bring those experiences and lessons learned with them. One of the most dangerous statements is, "I'm a quick learner; I can figure out almost anything." Top level executives are brought in to show the team how it is done, not to figure things out in the process. By narrowing down your expertise, you will expand your opportunities. By including all of your successful experiences, you will show that you have done it before and can show them how. This will also help you avoid narrowing your expertise down too much.

We worked with an executive who came from the insurance industry and based on her resume, her profile, and her conversations with us, the only thing we knew or could remember was that she was a high-profile executive and board member in the insurance industry. What was missing, and came out about forty-five minutes into a conversation with her, was that she had completed fourteen merger-and-acquisition transactions, plus ten additional ones in which she had gone through the due diligence process and decided it wasn't right. She had been in a leadership role and gone through more deals that didn't go through than most executives, in one way or another, throughout their entire careers. This was missing from her conversations and online footprint.

Social Media and Your Online Footprint

Entire books have been written on this single subject. Rather than try to squeeze in a quick tutorial that wouldn't do justice to the possibilities, we'll focus on the question, "Do I really need it?" and a few things to keep in mind.

Social media is helping people build their own private portfolio. Companies are able to begin building trust prior to meeting or being introduced to you. They can see common contacts, a range of your content, and your personal/professional interests. As a result, there is an initial connection.

The rise of LinkedIn is a great example of this. LinkedIn has become one of the largest staffing companies and networking sites in the world. How is this possible when most LinkedIn profiles have less work experience background on them than the average resume? For users, the site offers information beyond their work background. Not only can you put forth your expertise, skills, and experience online, but also recommendations and endorsements from other people. You also gain access to groups and online communities.

Social networking sites are hot spots for professional work-related activity with a rapidly increasing user base. Establishing your presence on the web can be highly beneficial for your brand. Start by creating and maintaining an updated and comprehensive profile.

You can create a personal brand using social media networks. You have the power to control what people see when they search your name on Google or Bing. By creating profiles on sites like Twitter and LinkedIn, you can control what information is shown and what image you present.

When somebody visits your website's home page, he or she should be able to know instantly whom you serve and what type of impact you can make. This is "credibility and context." If people know what you do and why you are a credible authority, they are more likely to recommend you. Nobody wants to be embarrassed with a bad recommendation that puts their judgment into question.

By using social media sites, you are making it easier for people to recommend you. This is important; the more consequential strangers who know what you do and can tell their friends what you do, the more likely they will be to refer business to you. This strategy does not depend on whether you have a large or small social network, but on how effectively you communicate what your business does.

Websites

We often hear the question, "Do I need a website?" A company has to have a website. Otherwise, some clients will think you don't exist or are not substantial enough to do business with. This doesn't apply as broadly for independent executives. When building trust, it can be helpful to more quickly build validity. Because so many executives don't have websites and instead are using social media, a website can help you stand out. It also can show your commitment to working as an independent executive as a career and highlight the areas you focus in. Given how easy building a website is, with drag-and-drop sites on the rise, it doesn't take much. It is a simple way to establish an online presence.

Pictures

Please make sure your headshot is professional. No pets, children, fishing trip, or NASCAR weekend. As pretty as the beach is, it doesn't come across as professional. We have had clients comment on this. They do like to get to know you on a personal basis, but an unprofessional or inappropriate picture can leave a bad image in the mind of the client or referrer. You don't want that image to be remembered as you snuggling with your dog rather than the image they want of the person who can help them with their company.

Pulling It All Together

There are an infinite number of options for creating and communicating your brand. It starts with your background and ends with your client's needs. As challenging as it is to find the shortest path between the two, it can be one of the most effective things you can do to set yourself up for success.

— CASE IN POINT —
Using Your Client Base as Your Brand

Whitney Vosbough views his entire career as independent, given the work arrangement or limited tenure of his roles. The longest he has ever worked in a single role was for thirteen months after his wife bet him that he couldn't stay in one place for more than a year.

At one point, Whitney decided it was time to start building a track record for himself. He knew the best way to do that was to work with some of the bigger names early on. He started with paid summer internships at major newspapers. He went from working as a graphic designer to creative director and then became a brand consultant. From there, he took a position as an interim VP of marketing, and then interim chief marketing officer for startups. Along the way, he did some big corporate interim jobs. After working with a large percentage of the past and current Fortune 500, he decided to take his extensive professional background and focus in on a very narrow marketplace—Interim CMO for Fortune 50 companies. Rather than focusing on marketing or industry-specific expertise, Whitney has built a collection of expertise that specifically resonates with Fortune 50 companies.

By focusing on the size of the company rather than the industry or specific situation, Whitney's applicable experience, and parallels are more relatable within his field of expertise. For example, he was recently interviewing for a consulting CMO role at a Fortune 50 company. He was asked, "Are you familiar with large enterprise culture and organization, the roadblocks, and the constraints that come with that hugeness?" He answered, "Yeah. Sure. I've consulted with companies like Chevron and Merrill Lynch as an on-site interim executive. I very much understand, not just from one point of view but from a multiplicity of points of view, what the reality of working within a large matrix legacy enterprise is." The industry didn't matter but the relatable experience did.

Whitney's advice to independent executives building their book of business is to volunteer. Work for free. Use it as a learning experience. If you do the right learning, you will get the right earning. The learning comes before earning. Know what your core purpose is. What are your core values, and then what is your core value to others? What is your gift? What is it that you do that few others do as well? Because when you're a consultant, you're going to be thrown curve balls all day long, day in, day out. You have to know how to swing with those curves.

Whitney recommends making an inventory of everything you've ever done and keep adding to it. This includes professional and personal experiences. It will help you in numerous situations, including those bridging-the-gap questions in terms of "do you have experience in/with so on and so forth?" You can't imagine the impact of a good story.

— CASE IN POINT —

No More Cold Calling—The Referral Black Book

Joanne Black spent much of the early part of her career in training and development, either managing or selling high-profile training programs. Each role was greater than the next, and she saw each as an amazing learning opportunity. She was fortunate to be referred into each role and learned to pay attention to what was going on around her and identify opportunities that made sense.

When Joanne decided to start her own company, she thought through what she had been doing for the past decade. She worked with companies of all sizes, and she noticed a common theme. Companies had business plans, but the sales plan was buried someplace in the larger plan and easily got lost. In most small companies, the founders typically have no sales background. Most of them have technical skills, or they come from finance, research and development (R&D), product development, or marketing; very, very few come from sales. They don't have a sales strategy with their go-to-market position. What's the value of their offering? How are they going to communicate it? Using the process and techniques that she had developed selling consulting and training to these companies, she decided to work with companies focusing on their sales strategy.

Her very first client was a referral and they needed help developing a sales strategy. They were doing a customer satisfaction survey with fifty of their best clients. Joanne added a question that had not been in prior surveys. "Would you be willing to be a referral for this client?" She can't recall why she asked that question, but it was a seven-point scale. Seven was high.

The results came back a six-point-five. So, this company asked fifty of their best clients if they would be referrals for them. There they are. Were they asking? No.

That was Joanne's "aha moment." She'd been selling and managing sales teams her entire career. Her best business had always come from referrals. She was paying attention to what she was seeing and knew there was something more there, so she started talking to salespeople and asking if they liked to get referrals. They gave her the same answer then, twenty years ago, that they give her today. "Yes! We're presold. They know us. We have trust. We have credibility. Our sales process is shortened. Our cost of sales plummets. We win deals from the competition, and we convert prospects to clients well more than fifty percent of the time."

Okay, so that's great. The next question became, "do you have a systematic, disciplined referral program with strategy, metrics, skills, and accountability for results?" The answer was "no" twenty years ago, and the answer is still "no" today. The fact is, everybody says referrals are great, and they happen, but companies don't have referral discipline. Joanne needed to figure out what was going on. If referrals are so great, why aren't companies pursuing them? Why aren't referrals their number one outbound prospecting strategy?

Joanne then leveraged her background and structured a very simple, straightforward referral program with key building blocks that have to occur before you can ever ask for a referral. What's interesting is that, twenty years later, those building blocks are identical. They haven't changed because the basic premise behind referrals hasn't changed. That's how Joanne has ended up working with companies on systematically getting more referrals. She had no initial plans for it, but like so many successful executives we have discussed throughout this book, she paid attention, did her research, and leveraged her background each step of the way.

Joanne was listening to what people needed. You don't just go create something because it's your passion; there has to be a need in the marketplace for what you have. There's even more of a need today, but the issues are exactly the same. The two major challenges every sales executive tells her they face are: number one, getting a consistent stream of qualified leads, and; number two, getting meetings with decision-makers. Now, there are a lot of others, but those are the two big ones.

Joanne had a lot of options when she started her business. She could have conducted sales training on just about any topic, offered sales assessments, been a part-time sales manager, and so on. Instead, she paid attention to the biggest pain point of her marketplace and zeroed in on what she saw as the top solution for it—training sales teams on a systematic and accountable program to get more referrals.

The advice Joanne gives is to test the offering. "Make sure there is a market for what you're selling. You need to get that reality check. You also can't look like everybody else. That could be something brand new, or it could be a twist on what you're already doing that is perceived as different. That's something people can resonate with. You need to continually listen to what the problems are. Unless you solve a problem, it's just like throwing spaghetti against the wall. You'll never be successful. It doesn't matter how passionate you are."

Joanne leverages what she does throughout her

brand. Rather than using the term "referral selling," she created her brand around the pain her clients experience and appropriately named her company, "No More Cold Calling." That is the foundation of her brand strategy, and everything else ties back to it. She actively engages social media as part of the strategy. The way people are having conversations today differs, so she is very active on social media. She posts regularly and ensures her brand is out there.

Many times, people know what their brand is. They just don't know how to position it, or they may be hesitant to really put it out there. Joanne's advice to someone who isn't sure is to hire a marketing/brand consultant to work with you to figure it out. We all get too close to our company, our message, and ourselves, and we need to have an outside expert help us. Know what you are good at and what you are not good at. Leverage what you are good at and get outside assistance for the rest.

YOUR BUSINESS COACH

1. Do you have all of your work, boards, and volunteering written down in one place?

2. How do past clients and coworkers describe what you do best (in their own words)?

3. In what areas would past clients and coworkers rate you four or five on a five-point scale?

4. What do you enjoy doing most?

5. How do you help clients and take their pain away?

6. What are your top accomplishments?

7. Do you use numbers to convey what you do?

8. What is your executive brand?

9. Do you have case studies, write articles, or speak about your area of expertise?

10. Have you registered at the executive online marketplaces that meet your criteria?

11. Is your online footprint professional and representative of how you help clients?

CHAPTER 4

Always Be Doing Business Development

Nurturing Your Business Sources

Too often, we see executives take on an engagement that is four to five days per week for a period of time and neglect their business development efforts during that time. Their efforts don't pick up again until their engagement is close to the end, at which time their previous efforts have lost their momentum. Out of sight, out of mind. If you only keep in touch with your contacts when you are looking for your next engagement, their ability to keep you top-of-mind decreases.

Business development is one of the most time-consuming, yet extremely important parts of being independent. At one time or another, every executive will be challenged with keeping a consistent portfolio of clients. Some of the more common sources for business are networking and referrals. We'll go into each in a bit more detail in this chapter.

Networking

Even though referrals are the number one source of business for independent executives, we are starting with networking since it often leads to the referrals. Networking doesn't necessarily mean going to event after event. The initial goal is getting in front of people and making new connections. Every person you meet is a connection and you never know where it might lead. Below are some of our basic tips for networking.

- **Choose Wisely.** Choose events that either have a topic you are interested in, someone invited you who can introduce you around, or are likely to attract client decision-makers. The third is fairly obvious, but can often be the least productive events without at least one of the first two criteria.

- **Ask Questions.** If you haven't read it in a while, pull out Dale Carnegie's *How to Win Friends and Influence People*[7]. No one likes going to an event and being sold to, especially CEOs. Some don't even like going to an event and meeting people. They go for the speaker, the topic, or because they were invited. Help to put them at ease in a conversation. Ask questions and get to know them. Whether they are potential referral sources or potential clients, you should end up knowing far more about them than they know about you. It is very off-putting when we go to an event where someone knows nothing more than what our company does, and we are handed a business card with the comment, "If you ever need my services, please call me," and that is the extent of the conversation. You'd be surprised how often this

---

[7] Carnegie, Dale, Dorothy Carnegie, and Arthur R. Pell. *How to Win Friends and Influence People*. New York: Simon and Schuster, 1981.

happens. Many of our clients don't network because they know most people they meet with either see them as a sales target or just tell them what they want to hear. That's not valuable to them. If you do meet potential clients, ask questions. Keep the conversation focused on them. If they can use your help, the conversation will turn into a discussion. Make a gentle offer, like, "I'm happy to provide some additional insights and expertise. Let me know." The more aggressive you are, the more it will turn them off.

- **Good Connections.** A good rule of thumb a friend once gave Kristen is, "If you connect with one person and schedule a follow-up meeting, it was worth going. If you connect with three people and schedule follow-up meetings, leave the event, because it doesn't get any better than that." That's the Rule of Three. However, beware of walking out with a handful of business cards and expecting results from just this one activity and a quick conversation. Do the follow-up. Initially, you will be more focused on quantity and meeting with as many people as you can. Once you get to know who the best referral source for you is (and vice-versa), you can be more particular about the types of people with whom you speak and follow up. Make sure they have the best chance of referring the right type of business to you or you are able to refer business to them. It's a two way street.

- **Research Speakers.** Do your research on the speakers and panelists, especially if they happen to be C-Level executives at companies that fit your target audience. The more you know about them, the more comfortable you will be having conversations with them after the event. Speakers always appreciate it when you come up to talk about them and what they said instead of what you want to sell them.

- **Have One-on-Ones.** Kristen's friend jokes about the Rule of Three, but in general, it is a good number to use. For each person with whom you connect and determine it is worth following up (hopefully for both of you), you will be scheduling a time to meet. Your goals for follow-up are: a) to learn more about each other for the purpose of determining how you can assist each other, and, b) to determine whether there is anyone else in your networks to whom you can connect each other. You will likely end up with one to three introductions from each of those three meetings. Think of it as rock-climbing. You step from one rock foothold to another and see where it leads, with the goal of ending up at the top of the mountain.

- **Explain Your Brand.** We have discussed at length about your brand and what you are the expert at so we won't go into it much more here. Stay consistent and stay focused.

- **Extend Your Network.** Another friend has a rule

when he's looking for work: never eat alone. He has every breakfast, lunch, and dinner scheduled with someone he's just met, or from his network. Basic math says that is fifteen connections/reconnections per work week. Using LinkedIn math, how many people are each of those fifteen connected to? By implementing this strategy, as long as you communicated effectively, you've just extended your network, too.

- **Follow up.** If you say you will do something, get it done right away, not a week later. This is part of your brand.

- **Connect and Reconnect.** Use your marketing tools. Get connected to each person you meet, whether you meet with him or her one-on-one or not. These are two basic ways to easily stay connected and updated (and vice-versa). Think of these networks as your mailing list/marketing database.

  – Send a LinkedIn invite (always with a customized message). Then continue to keep in touch with them on at least a quarterly basis reaching out with information that might be of interest to them, such as an article, blog, news, etc.
  – Follow the person on Twitter. If you aren't quickly followed back, send an e-mail follow-up and request a follow on Twitter, along with something that might be of interest, such as an

article you wrote or one you recently read and thought was interesting.

- Send an occasional e-mail with an article or blog that you wrote to keep you top-of-mind and that continues to demonstrate the types of areas you are a thought leader in.

- **Leverage Connections.** Follow and respond to updates/posts from your connections—send congratulations or endorsements and use them as a reason to stay top-of-mind or to get together. Send out updates on what you are doing; even if people just see your name, you can stay top of mind. Today, social media is your publisher. Get your message out across all digital sites (website, Twitter, Facebook, LinkedIn, Instagram, etc.). Even though most of your connections may not be potential clients, they may know people who might be. The more consistent you are with your brand, your messaging, and publishing, the more you will stay top-of-mind for the right reasons. And stay in touch. We cannot stress this enough. There are too many resources available to you not to stay in touch with people. Comment on something they posted, send them congratulations and a "let's catch up" note when they switch jobs, or send them a message with an interesting article. Entire industries have been formed around news aggregation. We have yet to have someone say, "Please don't share recent news or interesting articles with me." Even though they may not read them, doing so helps to keep you top-of-mind.

As your career ebbs and flows, you may focus on some areas more than others. In the current age of technology, in which 87 percent of consumers use more than one device at a time[8], attention spans are dwindling. If you want to stay top-of-mind, you need to be consistent in your efforts.

Kristen often tells the abridged version of how she and Pam met and got to know each other as members of a large nonprofit board. The punchline of the story is that they met through networking. As Kristen was making the transition from a full-time career executive to being independent, she networked, networked, and networked. Through about five different connections and working on an association committee, she was ultimately referred to a large nonprofit board where she and Pam then got a chance to initially work together.

Referrals

The most powerful marketing tools for any business are business referrals. People are inclined to trust business referrals if they come personally from somebody they know. According to research by Nielsen[9], 77 percent of consumers are more likely to buy a new product when they learn about it from friends or family.

Getting out the message about how great your business is

[8] http://www.adweek.com/lostremote/accenture-report-87-of-consumers-use-second-screen-device-while-watching-tv/51698
[9] http://www.nielsen.com/us/en/press-room/2013/global-consumers-more-likely-to-buy-new-products-from-familiar-b0.html

does not depend so much on the size of your social network, but on how memorable your brand is. You should be able to leave consequential strangers with a clear understanding of what you do, in just one brief conversation. To expand your reach, you want to give them enough information to further recommend you to their network, but not so much information that they lose focus on what to remember. Their recommendations can be quite valuable; they build trust with both the potential client and the referral partner. If the outcome is positive, it creates a ripple effect and word spreads.

So, what does it take to be trusted and recommendable? Establish enough credibility and context so that people know clearly what it is that you do. There are three steps to becoming recommendable so your network can be part of your business development department.

Stay in Touch

As nice as it would be to simply meet someone and have them immediately refer business to you, this is rarely the case. You could have worked with someone for years and they still won't remember to refer you. We can't stress how critical it is to stay in contact. There are too many sources available today, from e-mail to LinkedIn to the old-fashioned "pick up the phone and call." Often, what is now considered old-fashioned is the most effective, because it is so rarely used. It can be as simple as checking in to see how somebody is doing and what's new.

This includes contacts from years past. When you leave a company, whether as an employee or a vendor, you have built relationships with people who have a personal working knowledge of your work. They can be some of your most powerful referral sources. Follow their work moves and keep in touch. Make sure they know what you are doing. *Out of sight, out of mind* really does apply here. Stay in view consistently and your contacts will think of you first.

Be selective. Yes, you may have 100 people on your referral list, but only ten of them may actually ever refer you. It's really better to concentrate most of your outreach efforts on those ten. Help them out, stay in touch, communicate, and keep them updated on what you are doing. Just because you published an article, that doesn't mean they saw it. Send it to them. It may trigger something with one of their clients and make it easy for them to forward; this one activity can easily get your name in front of their client more quickly. LinkedIn can be used in the same way. Stay in touch with your network. Posting articles, publishing thoughts about someone else's article, etc. Get out there as a thought leader. You never know what may trigger a referral.

Continually Expand

Never stop expanding your referral base. Although the number of new people you meet on a weekly or monthly basis may slow down as your business matures, make it a point to get out and meet new people. For those who have a difficult time doing this in person, there is nothing wrong with building up your online referral base. It is always best to strike a balance between the two, though. If you aren't expanding your social media networks by meeting new people in person, set a goal to connect with a specific number of people each week. Even on Twitter, some of the most unlikely people may know someone who could use your expertise. You just never know, so don't judge too quickly.

Your Executive Brand: Be Memorable

We will reinforce this over and over: no matter how many people you meet or connect with, they first need to remember you in order to refer you. Ask yourself, "what do I want to be remembered for?" As we have previously discussed, contrary to most instincts, the more you niche your expertise, the more you will get referred. Why? Simply put, a specialized skill set is easier to remember and makes it easier for others to recognize opportunities for you.

If either of us were to meet you and say, "I help CEOs bridge the gap between where they are at and where their company wants to be," how would you help refer us? It doesn't matter how many pictures of a bridge are on the business card; that doesn't help us as referral partners.

Another common statement we hear is, "I help drive revenues through innovation." Again, increasing revenues through innovation has become such a buzz phrase and broad topic, it does not help anyone understand what your expertise is and what you can do for them.

Imagine you are meeting someone for the first time at an event, and they ask you "what do you do?" The answer to this question should be one short phrase that effectively communicates your work. It can take this form:

"I help (your target market), facing (the situation they are typically in) to get results such as (an example of what you have done for a client)."

Fill in the blanks, and you'll have a one-sentence answer that helps make the listener understand and remember what you do. To boost in its delivery, you can rehearse it beforehand. Rehearsing a simple sentence might seem silly, but it can be one of the most powerful tools you have. Based on your audience's reactions and follow up questions, you will adjust it over time.

Keep it memorable. If a stranger you meet today cannot remember what you said enough to pass it on to someone they know or meet tomorrow, you aren't going to get any referrals. As contrary as it seems, the more you narrow your messaging, the more referrals you will get. Denise did a great job of this, especially in the beginning, when she was networking and trying to find a way to be more memorable.

Remember Denise and the successful career she has built as an independent executive: her passion is productivity. When she looked back at her career and made her list, everything she had ever accomplished for a company tied back to productivity. To make herself memorable, she took on the title "Queen of Productivity" and used two or three numerical examples to illustrate how she had saved or made companies money. Every conversation she had centered around productivity and her questions supported it. Even online, she tied everything together in a memorable way with productivity scenarios and stories. Every time someone sees her name, it is accompanied by an article, tweet, or meme about how a company or individual can become more productive; the theme is continually reinforced. The moment someone in her network hears a CEO talking about productivity or related topics, like accountability, they immediately think of Denise. They may not think of her if the company is having an issue with inventory, which she certainly can help with, but she'd much prefer referral partners to remember her ten times for productivity than once for three other things.

Past Clients and Past-Client Referrals

One of the most important activities you can engage in is to contact prior companies and clients. Nobody knows better what you can do than those for or with whom you have already worked. We are increasingly seeing companies bring on executives who have worked with them in the past on a consulting basis. Keep in touch and reach out to them periodically.

Kristen was recently talking to the owner of a technology services company. The company was very niched, with a target audience of marketing personnel. As the owner explained, the problem for marketing departments is having minimal or no access to IT resources. His company is able to provide them with dedicated IT resources, a technology team that understands marketing specifically, ways to make their lives easier, and what they do more effective. His comment was, "Our clients love us—we help make them heroes."

As powerful a statement as this is, he had rarely kept in touch with past clients. So, he went through the exercise of contacting past clients. For almost half of his clients, the original marketing contact was no longer with the company. He reintroduced himself and his company to the new marketing personnel and brought them up to speed on how much of their technology his team had put in place. He then went online and got in touch with all of the former contacts he had worked with.

Almost one-third of the contacts he connected with mentioned how frustrated they were currently and wished his team was onboard to help them. Within the first month, he had two new signed contracts.

Similarly, your past clients can be your most powerful source of referrals to other companies. Never assume that because you worked with them for six months, they will automatically remember you for the next project. They could have the exact same project needs and still forget to contact you. If reaching out regularly does not come naturally to you, put together a schedule and identify whom to connect with on a quarterly, semi-annual, or annual basis. Get it onto your calendar and reach out when the reminder pops up; no hitting the "snooze" button.

Be a Referral Source Yourself

When you're communicating with your network, remember to go beyond what you want and need and look at what you can do for others in your network. Careful not to focus so much on finding opportunities for yourself that you miss opportunities to connect and help other independent executives. Helping others, whether they are your clients or your referral partners, is one of the most powerful brands you can build.

How to weed out and zero in on the best referral sources can be a struggle, but can also provide more value than you think. Who are the people to whom you are willing to refer? What is their niche? Did you do due diligence on referral sources to see whom you'd be willing to refer? This is important because it can have an effect on your brand in many ways. You want to build two-way relationships with people who will have a positive impact on your brand.

Partnerships

We will go into this in more detail in chapter 10, but we think it is important to also include it when talking about referrals because they are one of the biggest drivers of partnerships. From strategic partnerships to joint ventures, creating some type of formal or informal referral partnership is a growing trend among independent executives. This can be especially useful when you are bringing in common expertise to complement or supplement what you are doing for your clients. For example, as an operations executive, Denise finds that many of the clients she works with are challenged with legacy systems and are unable to easily create the reporting and visibility they need. She likes to bring in a technology consultant to assist. After working with the same technology executive on more than one engagement and seeing how well their work complements each other's, it may make sense to set up a referral partnership. This type of informal referral relationship is how Cerius began.

Optimizing Your Business Development Efforts

Because your time is limited and you will want to start narrowing your efforts at some point, put in place some basic due diligence on each source, just as you would with most other things. As you start to experience lead generation from various sources, you may notice patterns. For example:

1. You may find that specific sources don't lead to the type of work you are looking for—smaller, project-based work versus interim, longer-term engagements.

2. Your strengths may end up playing better to some sources than others.

3. Your time from introduction to starting the engagement may be shorter versus longer for some sources.

4. Your up-front time investment may vary between sources. For example, it may take longer to gain trust and get to know a client you met through social media efforts versus one who was personally referred to you.

The good news is, compared to ten years ago, there is now a full range of options. Keep your hands in all of the baskets and try out each one until you learn enough to decide where it makes the most sense for you to focus your efforts.

Pulling It All Together

As daunting as it may seem, there are a variety of approaches and opportunities for building your business as an independent executive. Step back and think about what advice you would give CEOs for building their business. Treat yours in a similar fashion. When it all comes together, you will see how easily the building blocks start to fit together.

— CASE IN POINT —

Knowing Your Audience

Steve Kerler has been independently consulting for more than fifteen years. In his career, he has worked with more than sixty clients, mostly in the Fortune 500, across twenty industries, in eighteen-plus different business functions. He ran the western United States division of a global consulting firm and has been an independent executive several times in his career. So, what can those of us who didn't take that path and don't have decades of consulting background learn from his experiences?

Like many, Steve was a senior executive who was laid off during the post-2007 recession. He quickly began networking, met some people who were doing consulting, and found some projects he could help with. He was back working as a consultant, this time independently, and has continued doing so ever since. Steve really enjoys the variety of the work.

There was, however, one big challenge for Steve. He'd spent most of his career changing roles and consulting under the umbrella of a large consulting firm. How would he narrow down his expertise in terms of clients and how could he solve their problems? As Steve puts it, "That makes it very difficult. I think clients, mistakenly these days, are looking for that old purple squirrel that everybody talks about; they want to go very deep and very specific on needs."

Years ago, Steve got some advice from someone he thought could sell ice to an Eskimo. Steve asked him one day, "What makes you successful? What's the magic sauce here?" The friend said, "Steve, it's really easy. All things being equal, people buy from people they like, know, and trust. All things not being equal, people buy from people they like, know, and trust. That's it."

That answer really stuck with Steve. Now, twenty years later, he finds it couldn't be more true. Once you start practicing building trust with people through stories and through your experiences, they will grow to like you, trust you, and then want to hire you.

Instead of going into a sales pitch or a conversation and just talking about your technical capabilities and your resume, start using words that resonate with the client's problems and empathize what they're feeling on the other side of the table. You've been there. You've sat there.

Steve tells this story: "I remember one large

presentation I did. We won a $30 million deal with the City of San Francisco. I was one of four people on an oral presentation team. We had a bunch of technical people up there talking about all these wonderful detailed technical things that were frankly making the audience's eyes roll. Our presentation lead whispered to me in the middle of the meeting, 'Steve, you need to finish this off for us. This is going downhill fast.'

"I went up, and my talk at that point turned impromptu. I said, 'Look, all of you sitting at that end of the table. I've been there before, and I know right now your eyes are rolling. It's obvious we've got people here who really know their stuff. You may not have understood a lot of this, but you've got to walk away knowing that we also know our stuff. You've seen a whole list of clients we've done this for before, so you know we have the experience. At the end of the day, like you, I'm sitting in your shoes, thinking of the four firms you've just evaluated. Who would I like to work with? Who would I trust to do this?'"

Steve turned the conversation around to empathize with where they were at that point and related to that. They won the deal because the customer felt a sense of comfort that his firm could do the work without giving them a lot of technical speak. Connecting from their perspective was key.

Steve has created a successful business by rethinking who his customer is and who could benefit most from what he has to offer. Steve developed a channel of small- to medium-sized partner firms that don't have the bench to staff people with his expertise full time, so they bring people in on a 1099 basis for certain projects. As it is with many companies, they would get business, celebrate, then turn around and worry about how they were going to get the project done. Steve has developed a brand that addresses these clients' biggest problem: Keeping their clients happy. They know they can trust Steve to get the job done. If the work isn't in his comfort zone, he recommends someone who is right for it. If it is, they have confidence that he can take all the experience he has, pull it together, and add value, to the point at which the clients are happy and asking for more.

Steve used his background to understand his audience and found a way to leverage his wealth of experience and longstanding career in the industry. He created a brand that solves problems for both the companies he serves and the larger consulting firms who use his services.

YOUR BUSINESS COACH

1. Are you selective about the networking events you go to?

2. How many one-on-one meetings do you have per week?

3. What is the one thing you want someone who meets you for the first time to remember?

4. Do you categorize people in your network by how often you should keep in touch with them?

5. How often do you keep in touch with past clients?

6. Are there other executives or service providers with whom you can connect with for events, speaking opportunities, referrals, and engagements?

7. How often do you refer people from your network?

8. Are you always doing business development?

9. Are you leveraging your marketing and branding in your business development activities?

CHAPTER 5

Create a Relationship, Not a Client

Sell What You Can Do, Not Yourself

People are always more comfortable selling something or someone besides themselves. It's human nature. Many people just aren't comfortable selling period. We'll go into detail in this chapter, covering the range of sales situations, including getting past the initial hurdles of selling yourself, building a partnership with clients, managing client expectations, challenges, and rates.

Let's start with a common myth—you do need to be able to sell yourself to clients and referral partners.

Think of your background and the impact you have on companies as your product, not you. When thinking through it, take you out of the equation and use your company name, such as JKL Solutions, rather than your own name (for example, Jeanne K. Long). If you are challenged with this, make it a little less personal initially: think of yourself as talking about a friend or a company. Focus on the relatable experience, activities, actions, and results of JKL Solutions rather than those of Jeanne K. Long.

Don't Sell; Tell a Story Instead

Using a story about a similar company you have worked with, start telling a prospect what was happening in that company at the time, how you were a part of it, the great team you had, and the results you achieved at the end of that engagement. Make sure you describe the formula that made the team so great, because when you go into a new client, sometimes you aren't able to duplicate the same results because it will be a different team, different decision-makers, and different culture. Mentioning the team you worked with can also keep you from sounding as if it was just you who fixed the issues at that company. Ego and taking credit for everything rarely goes over well when selling yourself and your services.

Building a Partnership

For some executives, the sales process is seamless and comes naturally. For many, however, it is neither seamless nor natural. It is a painful process that seems like it never goes anywhere or drags on forever. If you are in that group, we've put together some guidelines for you to pick and choose from as you formulate your own process and style when working with clients, from due diligence to introduction to engagement.

For starters, stop thinking of it as a sales process and more of building a partnership. When we surveyed CEOs and asked, "when faced with a challenge or opportunity, what stops you from hiring a management consultant or interim executive," the top response was, "Trust—Believing they can do what they say they can do." When building a partnership, you need to establish credibility and reliability in order to create trust.

Your First Meeting Is Not an Interview—Listen to Your Client

Practice reading people. Really listen; ask the questions that are important to the client and work to understand the pains they are having. If you don't, they will likely end up talking about something that is not really the issue. Listen carefully and key in on what they are meaning to say, not just what they are actually saying. When answering their questions, again listen, and answer them directly. Stay on point as much as you can. Make sure that if you tell a story, it is relevant. Tell a story about a client or past situation that is similar to this client's situation and focus on how you resolved it together with the team. This will be really helpful to them. We have seen executives who struggle to connect with clients or bridge the gap between their experience and what clients need have greater success using this technique.

Do Your Due Diligence

As much as you want business, not all leads are created equal, and neither are all companies. Each company and situation are unique. As much as the company will be doing due diligence on you, you should be doing the same. Not every opportunity is right for you, and not every company is a good client. Think of conversations with the potential client as doing due diligence rather than an interview. Your goal is to get quality client leads, not just quantity.

Due diligence is an easy way to get information. Take the time and do it. Don't leave anything out. Review potential clients' social media, websites, blogs, etc., and also Google them to see what comes up. You may find information to help you connect and stay in touch or something that may cause you to question whether you want to do business with them at all. For example, Denise had a situation with a potential client in which the company really needed help and she was excited to work with them, but while doing some up-front research, a social media site called Glassdoor raised some red flags. It was heavily weighted with employees complaining about the company—more than one would expect. The challenge was that the company had never brought up any internal issues. The company didn't even know this information was out there. This actually helped reframe the priorities and work to be done.

Start with everything you can find out about the company, the executives, and who specifically you will be meeting. Between the Internet and the source of the lead, you should walk into the first meeting with a lot of information on the company. If you aren't familiar with the industry, include that in your initial research. This is a great time to connect with someone in your network who works in that industry. There is nothing more frustrating to a client than being asked questions the executive could have easily answered through some basic research. If your approach is to ask confirming questions to compare their answers with your research, let the client know up front that you'd like to make sure you have all of the facts straight.

Initial Meeting Goals

Your goals for the first meeting are:

1. To determine if you are the right fit for what the client is looking for

2. To determine if this is a client and/or engagement you want

3. To understand the client's situation, what they need, what they are looking to accomplish, and what types of results they are expecting

4. To get as much detail as you need, because you will need this information for your Proposal/Statement of Work later, along with deliverables and timelines.

The last goal is by far the most involved and may sometimes take multiple meetings if:

- The client is not used to having these types of conversations

- This is a big move for the client and they are working towards building trust with you

- The responses have not been very concrete or clear

- You have follow-up questions

- You are receiving contrasting pieces of information from various people with whom you have met

- Your first meeting is with a "qualifier" like a clerk in HR or an assistant and is not in the best position to be giving you the detailed information you need to qualify the lead

Think of these first meetings as discovery and planning discussions. The goal is not for you to rehash your resume and answer the client's questions. To accomplish the goals outlined above, they should be active discussions, with the potential client doing most of the talking. As the client explains situations similar to those you have dealt with in your past, share those stories. Explain the similarities, what you did to help, and the impact you had. Stay in tune with what the client is saying and keep the discussion relevant. The same goes for any questions you are asked. Answer the question you were asked; don't get sidetracked to a point you want to try to get across. Through an active discussion centered around understanding and planning, the client will develop a better sense of your abilities and begin to trust that you can help them.

Stay focused on the client's situation at all times and begin thinking about how you might solve that issue. This approach turns the tables on CEOs. We have seen their entire demeanors change during meetings like this. Clients appreciate when executives have done their homework and are truly interested in helping them solve their issues. Let the CEO do the talking while you guide the conversation toward planning and solving rather than facts and statistics.

Be aware of the number of initial meetings the company asks of you and your up-front time investment. Depending on the size of the company and the engagement, you may need to have separate meetings with various stakeholders, either due to their availability or simply because it's part of their process. Be cautious of meeting with the same individual(s) more than two times, and ask yourself, are the meetings focused on information needed to scope the engagement, or have they strayed into actually beginning the engagement? (We'll discuss this in more detail later in the chapter.)

Get Information as Early as Possible

Three of the most important questions to clarify up-front are budget, process, and timeline. Too often, these are left undiscussed until the end, when too many surprises can arise.

- **Budget.** Even though most of the time, your clients won't reveal (or know) their budget up front, always ask. If they don't know it, ask how they will determine it. Do your best to understand what their thought processes are regarding budget and keep them as part of the ongoing conversations until you get an answer.

- **Process.** Most clients do not have a process in mind for scoping a project and vetting an executive, and they will appreciate talking it through with you because this will likely be the first time they have thought about it. Details will include who else they would like you to meet with, who the decision-makers are, and who the influences are (who will have input).

- **Timeline.** Most often, clients have a timeline in mind regarding when they would like to start. Find out about any potential delays in the process, e.g., vacations or conferences that could delay getting meetings scheduled. If they are unable to answer with a general timeframe, ask, "How soon do you want to get what we have discussed accomplished?" and work backward from there.

Client Discussion: Getting It Started

Whether you are a novice to the process or have been doing this most of your career, everyone has their own spin and techniques that work best for them. For executives who are looking for insights on what others ask or think their current technique may need adjusting, below is a brief overview of common questions independent executives walk through with clients. Let these be a guide, not a script.

Weave these questions into the conversation. Don't do all of the talking, and try to go through only the questions that apply to the client's situation. When the discussion is one-sided, it is more difficult to bond. Instead, listen to their pains and bring up appropriate questions that will help you better understand. Give them a chance to talk about themselves and their company. They need to know you are listening to what they are saying.

Let's take James as an example. James was going to be meeting with a client, so he did a lot of research about the company and the owner. When James got to the meeting, instead of listening, he immediately went into a whole monologue about how much he knew about the client. The client was not impressed. First of all, he was not given a chance to talk. Secondly, he wanted to discuss how to grow his company to the next level; he didn't want to hear James brag about how much he knew about the client and his company. Needless to say, it did not go well. The owner later bonded with another executive who did listen to him.

Conversely, Denise had a CEO client who had a very short attention span and did not want the meeting to go over an hour. The CEO had never hired outside help and was nervous. The meeting ended up lasting more than two hours. The client was so engaged in the conversation that she barely realized that two-and-a-half hours had already gone by. It was a seamless conversation between Denise and the CEO. Denise even used future-oriented language during the meeting, such as, "Next week, we can start working on what you just mentioned."

How an executive comes across to the client is extremely important. The initial conversation can make or break future meetings, even if you aren't meeting initially with the decision-maker. Although the person you are speaking with may not be making the decision, he or she often can influence it. The more natural and stimulating the conversation is, the more successful you will be.

When you are first starting out, sometimes the conversation isn't as natural as it could be. Below is an array of questions that can help you jump-start the conversation.

Once it starts to flow, you can then reference your list at the end to see if anything was missed.

- **General Questions**

  "Tell me how you started the company" or "Why did you decide to take this position?" This can help set them at ease with easy discussion and the history of it might become important.

  - What's the history of the company?
  - What's the history of the current CEO?
  - Describe your company culture for me. This question allows you to see the company's core values.
  - In ten years, what is the headline story of the company?

- **Future Plans and Goals**

  - What are the goals for next year?
  - What are the goals for company long term?
  - Where do you want to take your company?
  - How big do you want to grow your company?
  - In what period of time do you want your company to grow to that size?
  - What would you do with $1 million? This question lets you see if they have a single key predictive indicator; if they invested in this area, would it contribute this much to the company? Also, it lets you know if they have a weakness they want to shore up or an opportunity they want to push.

- **Current Status**

- What one word would your customers use to describe your company? This helps you to understand why customers buy from them and what emotional connection or brand connection the company has with its customers. Also, ask why customers would buy from them versus competitors.
- How are they different from other businesses/competitors?
- What are they looking to achieve if they had extra expertise? What type of expertise would that take?
- Do they hold trademarks, patents, or licenses?

- **Leadership**
  - How would you rate your management team? As, Bs, Cs, Ds, or Fs? If they say everything is fine, ask them to use the following criteria: "Knowing your managers now, would you rehire them?" Different answers may come out.
  - How would the company run without you? This tells you whether the person is in the business or leading the business and whether the leader has the right people who can and will make great decisions.
  - How does your management team know at the end of the day/month/week whether they met their goals? This tells you whether they have dashboards, focus, and alignment.

- **Needs in Your Specific Discipline**

  For example, if you are a finance executive, you are looking to understand more detail on who the players are, how it works in the client's environment, how it supports the business as a whole, and so on. Many times, you'll gain more insight through how they answer and what they focus on rather than the details they share.

Managing Client Expectations

As mentioned above, a company brings in an independent executive because they want to accomplish certain goals. When you work with a CEO or company owner, you are often helping them accomplish a long-term vision, their hopes, or even life-long dreams. They are bringing you in because they need an expert to fill a gap which is often seen as the missing puzzle piece. It is wonderful to get into grand discussions of their vision and how you can contribute, but remember to bring it back down to earth when the need calls for it. Although you may have the specific role you will play and how you can contribute clear in your own mind, the client may be hearing, "this person will make it happen." A lot of factors play into accomplishing overarching goals. Be clear on what your contribution will be, what they need to do, and what outcomes can be expected in the short- and long-term. This is one of the biggest gaps we see when speaking to clients about past experiences with outside resources like independent executives. Expectations from clients far exceeded either the capabilities of the executive or the basic reality of the situation. Remember, according to the survey we did, one of your top business development sources will be referrals from past clients, so you can't afford to have even one unhappy client.

A lot of work and energy goes into getting a job done. So, it can be quite disappointing when the client isn't satisfied with your results. There could be a number of reasons for why a client is disappointed, but ultimately, it's because expectations were not matched.

How do executives manage client expectations, especially knowing that everything they recommend will not be accepted or implemented? What are some of the common pitfalls to avoid and recommendations that are essential to keep the ball rolling in the right direction?

Mismatched client expectations usually occur in one of the following areas: expectations and goals are not clearly defined and documented, something is overstated or over-promised, misalignment occurs, or there is a lack of visibility during the engagement.

Defining Expectations

Managing client expectations begins with defining them at the very beginning. It's the executive's job to make sure that he or she is on the same page as the client, and that expectations are consistent with those of the CEO, business owner, or whomever they are being held accountable to. A Statement of Work can keep executives focused on what needs to be done and offer initial clarity to the client.

When a client complains that an executive—whether

full-time, interim, or consultant—hasn't completed the job, that means that he or she didn't accomplish what the client expected. The executive may not have transformed the organization, but as long as the goals stated and agreed upon in the Statement of Work were achieved, the client should be happy.

Success starts with the Statement of Work. When the client and the executive are both clear and expectations are spelled out in writing, that is a good start. You know what the situation is at the outset and have a list of goals, deliverables, and a basic outline of how it will all be accomplished.

One of the biggest complaints we hear about management consultants is, "They didn't do the job they were hired for," or, put another way, "They didn't accomplish what I expected them to." Basically, they didn't meet the client's expectations. It falls on the executive to make sure they are clear at the start of the engagement and to stay on the same page throughout the engagement, despite continually changing business conditions.

This can be challenging, because most often, you are not brought into a company that doesn't have issues. Something is broken, some type of transition is happening, or the company is trying to reach some new level of achievement. Sometimes there are specific goals they have in mind, such as sales targets; other times, they are having a difficult time articulating what is going on, let alone where they want to go.

Overstating/Over-promising

In many cases, the independent executive is seen as a superhero who can come in and fix everything. In the client's view, just by hiring the executive, "my problem is going to be solved." Obviously, this is not necessarily the situation. It is deceptively easy for executives to put themselves into this position and start agreeing to and promising that they will get problems fixed. Simply using the phrase, "Don't worry, I can help," can easily be perceived by a client desperate to turn things around as, "I will fix everything; I've got it." But too many variables can affect the outcome, including derailing or destructive decisions by the CEO or business owner.

Get the full story and as much information as you can up front. Beware of agreeing to too much until you feel you have all of the relevant information, which may require a basic assessment first. Be cautious about making commitments and promises until you have all of the facts. As much as you would like to help and get the business, over-promising is not worth the negative impact it can have on your brand.

Misalignment

We noted earlier that it's important to be clear about the situation at the start of the engagement. Because business conditions can change so rapidly, it is important to document where they were at the outset and the reason the independent executive came in at that time.

Managing expectations requires focusing on the original issue for which you were brought in. Many times, executives get caught up in routine activities like attending too many meetings or outside activities (not listed in the Statement of Work) which can sidetrack them from the original purpose for which they were hired. This can also make them lose outside perspective, which is an asset to an independent.

Companies often don't realize how valuable an interim executive can be until they start the engagement. As time goes on and they realize this, the scope of work will typically start to expand. Keep any scope-creep documented and don't lose sight of the original goals. Do regular check-ins with the client to review the SOW as well as added items, the status of each, and make sure both parties are aligned or whether something needs to be adjusted. Situations change. Make sure you are monitoring those changes; better to address them during the engagement than to get caught in the turmoil of the aftermath.

— CASE IN POINT —

Staying On The Same Page

We worked with an operations and supply chain expert who went in and consulted with a client following an acquisition. There were four very specific objectives and deliverables stated on the SOW. In order to effectively accomplish the objectives, the executive needed to understand the strategic direction of the company. As it turns out, there wasn't one. The more questions the executive asked, the more the CEO enjoyed conversations on the topic and could see a strategy forming. More and more was asked of the executive and these conversations started to put a strain on his time.

As much as finding strategic direction became pressing for the CEO, the original four objectives were far more pressing for the day-to-day operations of the organization and the executive's performance on the original SOW. When faced with decisions about what should take priority, the newer strategic initiatives or the SOW items, the executive had to ask himself one question: "Three months from now, how will my performance be judged?" The company may have more clarity on its strategic direction, but if the original operational issues were not resolved, that would be the leading story about the executive's performance.

As much as it can be argued that strategy comes first, that was not the original purpose of the engagement, and the CEO was not willing to reprioritize it as such.

Lack of Visibility

Non-measurable results are not only difficult to achieve but also difficult to prove any progress toward. Clients are always more satisfied with results when an executive can give them numbers.

Rarely when we talk about results do we hear clients say, "I was ecstatic; he changed the morale in our company." Instead, they use numbers. "She increased my profitability by X; my revenue improved by Y; my employee retention increased by Z." Although they may recognize a difference in employee morale, that is not what sticks with them. It is not why they make recommendations. Keep track of accomplishments with numbers.

Most CEOs will provide access to this information because they also want visibility and, in most cases, don't currently have it. When possible, tie the numbers back to the original SOW or in your regular reporting. Though you may have discussed it during meetings, discussions are easily forgotten. Words and numbers are more easily remembered when they are written down.

Keep expectations tangible and aligned. The results you deliver might be good, but if they are not what the client wanted, that can cause serious friction in the engagement. Despite how much you may know an objective needs to be addressed, if it isn't a priority for the client, it can derail your engagement. If you're not delivering results that match the stated original goal, there's going to be a disconnect and some unhappiness there. Unfortunately, a bad experience is remembered longer and more intensely than a good experience.

Manage expectations and you can walk away knowing you did everything you could each time.

Rates

The question of how to charge (and how much to charge) is one of the first questions we hear from executives who are transitioning from being an employee to being independent.

The response to this question is, "It depends," and it does. What is right for each client situation can depend on a number of variables.

Hourly versus Daily

Hourly. If a company is hiring one of the Big Four consulting firms (McKinsey, Booz-Allen, Accenture, Deloitte) compared to a small, boutique firm or an independent management consultant, there is a big range in hourly rates, which start at $350 and go as high as $1,000, depending on whether entry-level consultants are working on the project or one of the partners. Generally, there will be a blend of resources who vary in rates. For a smaller, boutique firm, rates decrease considerably and will typically range from $250–$400/hour. Working directly with an independent consultant, the rates will come down slightly from there, starting at $100–$350/hour. When determining your base hourly rate, the age-old general equation is:

> Amount you want to make in one year ÷ 1,040 hours = hourly rate

Why 1,040? There are essentially 2,080 workable hours in a year (52 weeks × 40 hours per week). The rule of thumb is that most independent executives end up working about half of that, for any number of reasons, including the amount of time it takes to develop and get business.

For example, $250,000 per year ÷ 1,040 = $240.38 per hour, which is why so many consultants charge a typical rate of $250 per hour.

This can be a starting point as you process your rate and start to think about what you want to charge. Below are some considerations to then take into account.

Daily and Monthly. Interim and part-time executives generally quote on a daily or monthly rate rather than an hourly or fixed-rate project fee. Whether the executive works eight hours or twelve hours per day, the client pays the same daily rate. The same applies for monthly rates, whether there are twenty-eight days or thirty-one days in a month; the client pays the same agreed-upon monthly rate.

Because independent executives are tasked with achieving specific objectives and timelines, they are far less likely to get involved in day-to-day politics and minutiae. Thus, they may accomplish in three to four days what a full-time executive will accomplish in five days. Clients can then compare the cost of an independent executive working three to four days per week to what they would be paying a full-time executive employee (including salary, taxes, benefits, bonus, etc.). The cost will be close to the same, but the independent executive will get the work done faster. The simplified typical equation is:

$200,000 + 30 percent (benefits, taxes, etc.) + 20 percent premium (for the flexibility of using an executive temporarily or part-time) = $312,000 ÷ 52 weeks ÷ 4 days = $1,500 per day

Experience Level

Your experience level and what you have traditionally made as an executive will influence the starting basis for your rate. Be careful, however, with smaller companies, as you may not be able to start at the same basic rate for them; they simply won't be able to afford you.

Size of the Company and the Situation

We have discussed that potential salary level plays a factor in management consulting rates. Just as full-time salaries range based on the size of the company and the situation, so do consulting rates. Considerations can include both the company's situation as well as the consultant's situation. For example, a company turnaround will garner a higher rate than a project assessing a sales team. Some executives may also be willing to take less because they see an engagement as a fun challenge and are financially able to.

Length of Engagement

A project involving an assessment that will take two to three weeks will typically be quoted at a higher rate than one that will last three to six months. One thing to beware of is thinking that a full-time engagement for three months should be compensated at a lower rate than one that is part-time for three months. In reality, the fee should be about the same. Although there is more short-term income for the full-time three-month project, it might keep you from accepting another engagement for three to five days per week for more money.

We have talked to many executives whose usual fee is $2,000–$3,000 per day. That is reasonable when it is a short-term project or only a few days per month. In most cases, however, this doesn't work with larger engagements. When a client needs an interim executive for three to five days per week for six to nine months, do the math on what it adds up to. Does the total amount seem reasonable for the job you are being asked to do and the value of the work? Step back and look at the math from a few different perspectives. What are their other alternatives and the costs associated with those? How do those compare to what you are asking for in fees? How reasonable is $3,000 per day for a $30 million company based on what they are asking you to accomplish?

Availability

How busy you are (or aren't) can also factor into your fee equation. If you don't have any work scheduled in the next month and not much in your pipeline, you may be more willing to come down on your rates if you prefer some work to no work. Conversely, most interim executives have no problem standing firm on their quoted rate if they are busy and have a steady pipeline at that rate. Why work for less if you have prospective clients willing to pay you more?

Interest Level

Your interest level in the engagement can impact your rates. We have seen executives decrease their rates for engagements they are very interested in, and conversely increase them when there are elements that aren't as appealing, e.g., lots of travel or higher risk.

Fee Structuring

As you have seen, not all projects are created equal when it comes to how to quote fees for a project. The structure that is right for your situation will also depend on many factors. Typically, projects such as assessments and strategic planning can be done on a flat-fee basis. When there is a potential for a significant cost savings or revenue increase and the company has a small budget, adding a success fee combined with a lower-than-usual rate is something to consider. The right executive combined with an arrangement that fits the situation and client's budget can often make a big impact on the success of a company. We go into this in much more detail later in this chapter.

If you are working with an intermediary, remember to take into account the revenue split when you determine your pricing. Because they are taking on more supporting activities and work, you are able to spend more time working and less time doing business development.

To help illustrate all of the above, let's use Denise as an example. Denise's base hourly rate is $200 per hour. Two years ago, her base hourly rate was $175 per hour, but since she got so busy and was taking on a number of larger, new clients, she took that as an opportunity to test market a higher rate. Recently, she was referred to a client by someone in her network. After meeting with the CEO,

Denise determined this was the type of engagement she loved. It was a fast-growing company with a young team and a technically-oriented CEO. She really wanted to work with them. The company was going to need her at least three days a week to start, then likely at least one to two days per week for about six months. Using her $200 per hour base rate, she took into consideration that she was now looking at charging daily instead of hourly. The project would keep her busy for the next six to nine months doing the type of work she loved. She also knew the company was cash-flow-challenged due to its rapid growth. Denise came up with a daily rate of $1,200 and a success fee of 20 percent of her invoicing if the company reached its sales and gross margin goals at the end of the year. The CEO was thrilled to have someone of Denise's caliber on board a few days a week within a budget that worked for the company.

Client Relationship Challenges

If it weren't challenging enough getting the sales lead to begin with, you may face any number of additional challenges during your sales process. The more you are aware of them up front and address them as early as you can in the process, you will have more control over the situation than you would otherwise.

The Decision-Maker

As much as you may know better, it can be easy to get caught up working with someone other than the decision-maker longer than you should. What their decision-making process is, who will be involved, and who the final decision-maker is should be on your list of questions for the first conversation. When working with larger companies, it is common to work through most of the process with someone other than the decision-maker (for example, human resources). Get all of the information on the process that you can up-front, combine it with your experiences in similar situations, and decide whether this prospect fits your business model or not. Some executives know how to navigate larger companies, contracts, and processes well and are willing to take them on, depending on the size of the contracts. Others decide not to take on these clients unless they are immediately connected with the decision-maker and the process is fairly straightforward.

Sometimes you are working through your referral source—an informal intermediary—rather than being quickly and directly connected with the client. You are now reliant on second-hand information and follow-up. In our experience, executives are most successful in these situations when they work with the intermediary sooner than later to establish a direct connection to the decision-maker. Schedule time and brainstorm how to get you introduced as early as possible in the process. Usually, this is the case when the potential client has expressed frustration but isn't quite ready to resolve the situation. Your referral source can forward something tangible, like an article you wrote, that is pertinent to the situation and suggest an introduction. Continue to follow up with the referral source/intermediary, but be careful not to provide too much secondhand information.

Client is Nonresponsive

There are a number of reasons potential clients become nonresponsive, from other priorities coming up to not wanting to make a decision to having made a decision and not having the courtesy to get back to you. If you have received no response after a few follow-ups, we have seen the following e-mail succeed:

"There is a fine line between being persistent and being a pest. In order to not cross the line into the latter, this will be my final follow-up. Please feel free to contact me when you are ready to reconnect."

It is rare that executives don't receive a response of some kind after sending this.

Budgets and Fee Structuring

Fees can easily be the most contentious part of forming a relationship and can make the client unresponsive. Keep focused on what the client is looking to accomplish, the expectations, and the budget. Contracts can be structured a number of ways beyond project, hourly, or daily bases.

- **Success Fees.** If the company's budget is contingent on some financial return or success directly tied to your work, this fee structure can be a good alternative. Executives lower their base rate in return for a bigger upside when specific goals are reached. Outline the parameters and client expectations clearly, understand that some success is contingent on the client, and not everything is controllable. If you are willing to take a risk for a bigger upside, this could be a good option for you. Be sure the agreement contains assumptions and additional clauses to cover "in-the-event-of" items. For example, in the event the client cancels the contract prior to an opportunity to achieve the success fee, then what? Some of the more popular success fee arrangements are:

- Achieving X percent increase in sales or decrease in operating expenses
- Connecting the company with X number of strategic partners—because the executive is typically using his or her own network, there is an added success fee for setting up these relationships
- Preparing a company for sale—the executive receives a success fee of X percent of the increased value of the company based on the assumption the value increase is primarily due to the executive's leadership and efforts

- **Sliding Fee Scale.** In line with the success fee strategy, this structure starts at a fee below what you would normally charge given the circumstances, then increases, based on deliverables, goals, or time, progressing to a rate slightly higher than you would have received otherwise. You assume more risk in this structure than the client in many cases.

We suggest adding an extra clause to the contract stipulating that if the contract is terminated prior to the opportunity for increase, your normal rate would then be retroactive and due upon termination.

- **Deliverables-based Fees.** Some clients are very cautious regarding what value or deliverables they will receive for their investment. They likely have had a prior bad experience. This compensation structure is sometimes suggested by the client, but we rarely see it put into practice because trust needs to be a two-way street and most executives are not willing to take on most of the risk. Situations in which we typically see this fee structure are:
  - Executive gives extended terms of payment contingent on helping the client receive financing, secure a line of credit, or acquire X channel or strategic partners
  - Executive gives extended terms based on completion of deliverables

- **Retainers.** Some executives prefer being paid a month in advance and are willing to provide some flexibility with rates in these circumstances.

- **Reduced Work Week.** The client thinks they need someone five days a week; you know you can do the work in three, especially because you won't be involved in office politics, the water cooler, or excessive meetings. You will be more focused and can deliver more value for the same budget. In this structure, be careful not to be perceived as "overqualified." That may be interpreted as "too expensive; I don't need to pay someone that much," or "This executive won't be hands-on enough." Work through how you can make the same impact or more in less time. Provide examples of what you have accomplished in similar situations without being on-site full time. Story it!

When establishing your fees and payment schedule, don't diminish the impact of when you invoice and when payments are due. The service you provide is not one that can be returned. Once you provide the work, particularly deliverables, they typically can't be undone if the client doesn't pay. This is why most consultants prefer to be paid prior to performing any work in a new client relationship. Conversely, the client is in a similar situation. They are typically very cautious about paying for something prior to work being performed and particularly before realizing any value from it. As we have already mentioned, trust is a two-way street; you decide what is right for you in each client relationship.

Scope and Schedule Creep

Many clients are so happy to finally talk to someone of your caliber and expertise that the more you two talk, the more open they are with problems, issues, or opportunities, and the scope begins to expand. Part of your role is to help focus discussions and help the client clarify and prioritize what needs to be accomplished. Help the client understand the flow of your process and that it is better to accomplish a few things than to fail at a lot of things. Challenges with focus and priorities are likely one of the reasons the client contacted you in the first place.

We've had more than one client call with an immediate need, asking how quickly an executive can get started. And yet two months later, we are still dealing with scheduling discussions, finalizing scope, significant delays in responsiveness, or start-date delays. Including timeline information in your initial discussion and recapping it in writing can help to serve as a basis for continual communication on this topic. For example, "In our first discussion, you mentioned wanting to have X, Y, and Z in place by the beginning of Q1. It is November 1, and it will take at least eight to ten weeks to accomplish this. Have your plans or priorities changed?" Often, going back to the initial intentions and asking the question can help.

Too Many Discussions and No Action

How many times have you met with a potential client, and three meetings later you feel like you are no closer to moving forward with a Statement of Work than you were at your first meeting? A number of the suggestions already mentioned can help avoid this. Use your intuition and common sense. You will quickly start to identify those clients who love to meet and have discussions with you but will likely never move forward with an engagement.

This is your business. You decide how much time you are willing to invest and why. You should stay in control and make this decision, not the client.

Keeping clear communication and not hesitating to ask the difficult questions will keep you further ahead in the process. Look at it as building a partnership with the client, not a sales process.

Overcoming Common Objections

The Executive Must Be from My Industry

Through a recession or slow economic times, companies become accustomed to handcrafting lists of requirements for the executives they are looking for, from backgrounds to skill sets to the types of companies they have worked for in the past to "They must be from my industry." As the executive market gets busier and less talent is available, companies become a little more flexible about their executive wish lists. So, which items are easier for a client to be flexible about and still find the right executive? Does the executive really need to be from their industry?

It is not uncommon for an executive to transition out of a single industry after a long tenure and want to broaden their experience and activities. Here are some tips for talking through this objection with clients.

What Role Will the Executive Play?

Does the client need a VP of sales with established relationships and a network inside their industry, or someone who has the knowledge and ability to take their product into new markets or industries? What is easier to teach, the basics of the industry, or the right skill sets, culture fit, and relationships to increase growth in other areas?

What Kind of Learning Curve Does the Industry or Company Have?

Is the client a high-tech company that requires the knowledge of someone with an engineering degree, or a consumer products company in which a solid understanding of manufacturing and distribution (acquired from any industry) is enough to do the job? The learning curve is generally much less steep for the latter.

How Much of the Management or Current Executive Team Comes from the Industry?

Is the existing team a diverse mixture that can contribute knowledge and tenure from inside the industry and combine it with new and fresh perspective from the outside?

What Does the Client Need an Executive to Accomplish?

Why are they bringing an executive on board? What is driving the need for this person, other than to fill a title or a seat? Are they looking to outmaneuver the competition or just catch up? Are they missing high-level industry experience, or do they need fresh ideas and outside-the-box thinking? One option is to look at executives from industries with similar characteristics.

Inside the Industry: Pros

- Short learning curve

- Already networked inside the industry

- May be able to provide key insights (not proprietary information) from other companies for which he or she has worked within the industry

Inside the Industry: Cons

- If the executive is coming from a competitor, how will he or she provide you with a competitive edge that has not already been provided to your competitor?

- Lack of originality and thought processes beyond the industry

- Complacency

- Narrower pool of executive talent

A Perfect Example of a Key Executive from Another Industry

We had a client in the insurance industry with some brick-and-mortar service offices. Their goal was to increase revenues through these offices. They could not imagine anyone outside the insurance industry working with their teams.

We brought in an independent executive with a retail and quick-service food background instead. The company quickly saw how they could leverage the executive's background from outside the industry because he had overcome similar challenges in his own industry. The first year, the client company experienced a 20 percent revenue increase. (By the way, this was in 2008, when competitors were all experiencing a decrease.)

Being open to executives from other industries with attributes that a client needs just might help them hit the jackpot.

Overqualified

When it comes to an independent executive solving a company's pain points or helping them to reach growth goals, there is no such thing as being overqualified. The objection you will hear most often is, "too much horsepower for what I need." Roughly translated, the client is saying, "I don't want to pay that much for what I think I need to have done."

You can make effective counterarguments, including:

- By hiring an overqualified candidate, a company can bring innovation, efficiency, and maturity to the company, resulting in thousands, if not millions, of dollars in revenue, increased productivity, and cost savings.
- An outside perspective is invaluable in critical situations.

Focus on the initial reason you were brought in. Often, the list of what the client needs falls into two categories.

Using accounting and finance as an example. Most of the items on the list can be done by an individual at the controller level. A few items on the list, however, will best be handled by a CFO-level individual. As much as the company may want to find someone who can do both, they will likely end up disappointed in the end. This is the most common scenario we see. But in the end, if they aren't willing to spend the money and you aren't willing to work within their budget (which likely means accepting less than your usual rate), this strategy isn't going to work. The company will usually end up hiring a controller and bringing in a part-time CFO a few days a month.

Culture Fit

The client is worried about culture fit. It is not uncommon for executives to have gone through some type of culture or work-style assessment. Make your assessment results available and be willing to talk it through with them. These types of assessments are often not used as deciding factors, but rather as part of a pattern in the overall picture. The more you show the client consistency throughout your interactions, this will become less of a sticking point.

Red Flags to Watch For

- **Kicking the Tires.** Always beware when the potential client is vague about what they are looking for. Ask in-depth questions regarding where they are and what their needs are. Sometimes they are just kicking the tires and aren't serious about taking action. Make sure they really have a need and purpose for bringing in an interim executive.

- **Cost.** If all the client wants to talk about is cost, usually that means they can't afford to hire you. With large companies, however; this is common due to very specific budgets. One of your first questions should be, "what is your budget?" If the potential client is focusing on cost and budget and letting that guide the conversation, they likely can't afford your services. Beware of wasting your time.

- **Lack of Focus.** Even after talking for fifteen minutes, the client can't explain their needs well. This doesn't mean they won't eventually use your services, but expect a longer process, because they are at the beginning of their process. It may be a while until they reach the point where they are focused and know what they need.

- **Something Doesn't Feel Right.** If they are looking to get too much into the details of how you do things, or their questions aren't fitting into the conversation, listen to your gut. If something doesn't feel right, it likely isn't.

- **Signing on Behalf of Company.** Beware if the client asks if you have a problem signing anything. As an independent executive and not an employee, you should not be signing anything on behalf of the company because of the liability issues it could cause you. Ask questions and understand the reason first before jumping to conclusions but certainly a potential red flag.

- **Decision-Maker.** Your conversations are continually with people who are not the ultimate decision-maker; you are leaving the process to someone who may or may not know what they are doing.

Pulling It All Together

Rather than looking at sales as merely a process, consider it a journey between you and the client. Start with no specific destination in mind and work through it together. Keeping an open dialogue and establishing as much up-front as you can will help you avoid some of the most painful lessons learned by others that can have impacts far beyond a single conversation or engagement.

YOUR BUSINESS COACH

1. In your typical conversation with a client, what percentage of the time are they speaking versus you speaking?

2. Are you able to summarize their situation, their needs, and how you can help after the initial conversation?

3. What stories do you have from your past to convey to clients how you can help them?

4. Are you clear about the client's expectations regarding what you and your efforts can accomplish?

5. Are you keeping potential clients realistic about how you can help them and what can be achieved in their situation?

6. How early are you meeting with the decision-maker and finding out what the decision-making timelines and budget are?

7. What is your base hourly and daily rate? In what situations are you willing to be flexible?

8. Are you letting a client's sales process go on longer than you should?

CHAPTER 6

Establishing Guidelines and Getting Paid

We have referred to the statement of work (SOW) and its importance in terms of both the sale and delivery of independent executives' work for clients. How much or how little you put into yours is up to you and will depend on the situation and the client.

Creating a Statement of Work

Below is an outline we recommend, especially as you are getting started, to help ensure you are covering the basics.

Legal Sections

Most independent executives combine legal sections into the SOW rather than a separate document, such as a master services agreement. When working with larger companies, however, it is not uncommon to sign a vendor agreement separate from the SOW. The master service or vendor agreement covers the legal terms and conditions between your company and the client. A statement of work is specific to each project or engagement.

Situation

Businesses are living and breathing entities. They are continually changing, as well as their circumstances. The situation when you start an engagement can quickly change. Documenting the initial situation is a good reminder of circumstances during your final SOW discussions and can act as a reminder of the client's state of mind at that point. It is not uncommon for a client to question whether the goals, objectives, and deliverables are the right ones three months down the road. The challenge, in this case, can be that the circumstances or their perspective may have changed, and they are looking at them through the current lens. In some cases, the overall situation may be the same, but something happened recently and they are having a knee-jerk reaction. With a documented initial situation, you can revisit it to discuss whether it has actually changed and whether it should remain the focus of your efforts. The situation statement can include what is going on with the company, industry, and/or marketplace. What pain, issue, or vision the CEO has, and for what reason. Why are they seeking your assistance?

> **Example:** The company has been on a rapid growth cycle, but has recently fallen short of projected goals. Although the company is up 14 percent year-to-date, they are projected to fall short approximately 7 percent from plan. Management feels their salespeople may lack a successful process to develop new business and bring in new, targeted customers. The closure rate is below desired levels and management believes that the sales force should be more productive overall.

Your Background as It Applies to the Situation

This helps solidify in the client's mind that you are the right person to address the situation that has been described. Keep this section to two to three sentences.

> **Example:** Matthew has over twenty years of experience in the consumer products industry. His marketing and sales background within this industry will provide a comprehensive perspective of the market environment the company is in. Matthew has worked with over fifty companies and will be able to provide valuable insights based on an outside perspective to help the company achieve the below goals and objectives.

Goals and Objectives

The key point in this section is to get these approved in writing by both the client and the executive. Sometimes, it helps to put them in order of priority.

> **Example:** Company would like to double in sales (from approximately $21 million) in three to four years. This is a compound rate of growth of 19 percent–26 percent. In order to achieve this, management believes improvement must be made on identifying and closing high-potential target customers. They are seeking to identify and implement best practices and a process to accomplish their sales goals.

Scope

This section is a description of the scope of what you will be doing for the client and for what you will be accountable. Keep this section as realistic and clear as you can. Avoid making blanket statements that the client can easily interpret to include other items. You don't need to list your secret sauce and exactly how you will complete the scope of the project, but the section should be as detailed as you can make it, so as to not create unrealistic client expectations. List any dependencies and what you will need from the client on any items you feel might present a challenge or sticking point for them.

Example: The interim sales executive will work with the owners and current sales team to develop a sales strategy and process to achieve a sustainable increase in sales.

PHASE I. Sales Team Assessment and Discovery (Completion time: Three weeks based on two days per week)

1. **Sales team overview:** Review of the sales team members (meet with each person individually)
   a. Study account sales history, volume, and margin for each sales rep. Identify trends. See account turnover (new/loss)
   b. Interview: Meet with each rep individually to discover:

      i.   How they identify targets, approach, follow up, close

     ii.   Time reps spend on: Maintenance, support, or hunting; time with new or existing customers? Break down time

   iii.   Time killers (identify ways to eliminate)

   iv.   Their ideas on best ways to bring in and close new business. What is stopping them from achieving higher sales results?

     v.   How reps organize time and weekly schedule

   vi.   How reps set priorities

  vii.   Reps' view of sales compensation program and what would motivate them

 viii.   Reps' view of internal support

   ix.   SWOT on client versus the competition

    x.   If they owned the company, what would they do differently? Top areas for improvement to make it easier to focus on selling

  c. Brainstorm ideas for growth

2. **Shadow and Ride-along:** Travel with each rep to key targeted accounts

  a. Assess individual strengths and weaknesses

  b. Assess customer needs and requirements

  c. Identify how to improve client's sales process and customer experience to better meet the customer's demands.

Deliverables

At noted milestones or upon completion, is there anything tangible the client will have in-hand? List out what they can expect.

Deliverables should solve a pain the client has talked about. Look for low-hanging fruit that can quickly bring your client a return-on-investment in you. The client will always remember you when you save money or increase revenues enough to cover your fees. While going after quick wins, however, make sure you keep your eye on the longer-term goals as well.

Address the question, "Am I going to get something more than a report?" A deliverable is not just a report. It's your observations and suggestions for action. What are the next steps? How should the client move forward? What are some things the client can do based on their current resources? What actions would require additional resources? Include suggestions, estimated timelines, and expected outcomes. Otherwise, the client's response will be, "I already knew all of this." Give the client a roadmap and different options; they need the latitude to make a decision and not feel they are being forced in one direction.

We have seen some very successful executives say, "I can help you with these three projects, and here's how I would go about it." They immediately look for internal talent to assist in forming recommendations, and they leverage the team. This solves a number of pains for clients as well as offering spillover benefits.

Example: The overall objective is to increase productivity and close rate. To further this, report on and evaluate each sales rep's strengths and weaknesses. This report will detail opportunities for improvement for each rep as well as personnel changes (if recommended) and identify characteristics of the ideal sales person for the company.

Timelines

Always include timelines. Although they are sometimes difficult to predict, at the very least, provide a range, either within the scope by providing a timeframe for each task, or an overall range for when the client should expect all the deliverables. If timelines are based on client contingencies, list those to help hold the client accountable for the timeline as well. (In this example, the timeline was included as part of the Scope section.)

Start Date

As simple as this may seem, placing it in the SOW helps keep the client focused on your expectations to start. In the event the client does not execute the SOW by the start date, you cannot guarantee your availability or timelines. Including this sets an expectation with the client that your time is of value and you need to plan accordingly.

Communication and Reporting

Progress reporting and communication are among the most critical pieces to a successful engagement and keeping the engagement on track. This section may be as simple as stating there will be milestone updates or weekly/bi-weekly updates on each SOW item. In this example, reporting was covered as part of the Deliverables section.

Terms and Fees

Are you charging hourly, daily, or monthly? If you are charging a daily rate and the client needs two hours on an ad-hoc basis, how will these two hours be billed? Are you charging a retainer up-front in case they are slow to pay or stop paying you? If the work is a project, how much of the project rate is due and when? What expenses are preapproved, and up to how much? If you are being reimbursed for mileage, specify reimbursement will be at the current Federal Standard Mileage Rate. Your client should know exactly what to expect.

— CASE IN POINT —
Getting Creative in Terms of Fees

Companies are looking for executives who add value to the organization. Be creative with how you can help them as an executive. Stay focused on where the company wants to go and how you can get them there; it may not be obvious right from the start. Help provide solutions, including a creative success fee tied to goal achievement if you can. It should coincide with the direction the company is headed and help to get them there.

Denise is great at understanding what her customers need, what their biggest pain point is, and focusing first on that when she can tell a client is having a tough time moving forward bringing her in to help. When Denise was just starting out, a referral partner connected her with a potential client. The CEO identified a number of issues that needed to be addressed. One of her biggest was that her team was giving her recommendations and trying to force decisions she was unsure about. She had started to question her decision-making abilities which included her confidence as a leader. Although Denise had laid out a thorough, comprehensive plan to help address all of the CEO's needs and issues, she could tell the CEO wasn't going to make a move.

Denise took a step back and narrowed down the scope to the number one item that could help the CEO most—reporting. A lack of information and reporting had her leading the organization blindfolded. She didn't have enough information to question what her team was telling her. Denise adjusted the scope of the engagement solely to address this issue first. In just ten hours a week, Denise assured the CEO she would have the information, reporting, and visibility she needed in less than a month. This was an offer the CEO couldn't say "no" to. Four weeks later, Denise's client was so pleased with what she had done, they identified the next set of issues and needs for Denise to address. The scope was expanded and the client was thrilled.

The Back-and-Forth

In general, there should not be a lot of back-and-forth because you have been formulating the SOW with the client during your conversations and recapping each in writing. In most cases, adjustments to the SOW will fall under two categories: Scope and Fees. We often see clients either request the scope to be more detailed, adjust priorities, or include a few more things that have recently come up. Be sure to step back and read through it all carefully with each adjustment to ensure it is still consistent with the original intentions and that you can still deliver. Refer back to the Statement of

Work information earlier in this chapter for advice on how to address these changes in the development of the SOW.

Invoicing and Collections

This does not need to be complicated or fancy. Following are a few tips to keep in mind:

- **Professional**

  Your invoice should be professional and include all pertinent information. Whether you are creating it in a word-processing document or using a bookkeeping program such as Quicken or QuickBooks (desktop or online), it should look professional. Open and review each invoice before sending. Is your contact information on it? Are your payment terms and address on it? Yes, all of this information was included in the SOW, but accounts payable personnel rarely, if ever, get a copy of your SOW, so it should also be on your invoice.

- **Key elements of an Invoice**
  1. Date of invoice
  2. Payment terms and due date (make this as clear as possible)
  3. Logo (if you have one)
  4. Vendor name and address
  5. Client's name and address
  6. Description of service
  7. Quantity of units
  8. Units of measurement

9. Cost per unit

10. Extended cost (number of units × cost per unit; e.g., 2 days × $1,600 per day = $3,200)

11. Total amount due

12. EIN #

13. Make checks payable to

14. Wiring/ACH information (try to set up all of your clients on ACH payments; this will eliminate lost checks, and customers tend to pay faster if they pay their vendors via ACH)

- **Consistent with SOW**

  Ensure all information on the invoice is in line with the SOW. If your SOW terms are net fourteen and your invoice template says "due upon receipt" because those were the terms for the last client you invoiced, update it. As simple as it is to have one template, we have seen some pretty basic errors occur. The more mistakes you make on invoices, the slower clients are to pay you.

- **Delivery of Invoices**

  Although you may be working on-site with the client, send your invoice electronically. Paper is too easily lost, misplaced, or miscommunicated.

- **Description of Services**

  This depends on your personal style and the agreement with your client and can be as basic as a few words referring to your weekly update report or a detailed description of what was accomplished during the billing cycle. Focus on accomplishments, not a detailed accounting of your activities. You are not an employee. You are a vendor providing services as they relate to an SOW. Your description should reflect that accordingly.

- **Collections.**

  Manage your clients for invoice payments. Do not assume they got the invoice and are processing it. If payment is late, in most cases this is not done intentionally. Invoices simply get missed. You aren't always brought in under the best conditions, and those can include an overworked accounting department. Effective executives get ahead of issues and introduce themselves to the individuals processing their payments, either in person or virtually. Build a relationship. Let them know when to expect your invoices. Some are so great that they will contact you if they haven't seen anything come across their desk by the dates you gave them.

Pulling It All Together

They are not the most interesting part of the journey, but the SOW, invoicing, and collections help most independent executives stay in business and do what they enjoy. These can be as simple as you want, as long as clients have the information they need and you can track and collect your accounts receivable.

YOUR BUSINESS COACH

1. Do you have the appropriate legal sections as advised by an attorney included in the SOW or a separate Master Service Agreement/Vendor Agreement?

2. Are you including the "why" of the SOW—the background of the situation, not just what is to be accomplished?

3. Are the value and impact of your deliverables clear?

4. Does a specific client situation call for more creative terms and fees beyond the usual X amount per hour or day?

5. Have you talked through what to expect and an initial outline of the SOW prior to sending the final to the client?

6. How professional do your SOW and invoices look?

7. Collections are as important as getting a signed SOW.

CHAPTER 7

The Legalities

Nothing Can Take the Place of Qualified Advice

We are not attorneys. Although we have spent more money and time than we care to admit being advised by attorneys, insurance experts, and accountants, we have not been educated, trained, or certified in these areas of expertise. This chapter in no way constitutes legal, tax, or risk-mitigation advice and is intended solely for clarification and awareness purposes. For discussion and advice specific to your situation, contact a professional.

With that said, here is an overview of the information we have found to be most helpful and relevant to independent executives.

The Complications of Labor Compliance within the Independent Workforce

Gene Zaino, CEO and President of MBO Partners, is a thought leader on labor compliance and risk assessment. He offers a unique perspective on these topics:

> With the numbers of the independent workforce showing its might in recent years, the regulation and the legal implications are nev-

er far behind. When you think about it, our payment structure is what actually funds our government. Today many companies outsource their employment tax compliance to payroll processing providers such as ADP and Paychex. These businesses provide companies with built-in systems to help them easily pay their workers, and at the same time still be compliant with government regulations. The government gets its resources from our paychecks. We all know what our salary and our take-home pay are, and we know there's a big gap between the two. That gap funds your local, state, and federal governments. However, as more and more people migrate away from that traditional employment structure, our government is also becoming concerned.

The increase of independent workers has resulted in an increased level of enforcement of regulatory laws. There's always a need for the government to classify everything properly, and this includes people working in the independent workforce industry. As a result, it is up to the private industry to provide a structure that allows companies to be more independent and do their own thing, but still have an easy way to comply with government regulations. Tax collection and enforcement of tax laws aren't something that's going to go away.

But because one size doesn't fit all, you can't apply the same regulations and rules across the entire industry. After all, there are different types of contractors. There are people who want to be employees, but they are categorized as contractors because that's the way their industry works. Then there are companies that try to take advantage of people—instead of paying their benefits and taxes, they pay them as a contractor. This is why there is a need for regulation—as a form of protection to ensure that people get what they are entitled to, and to make sure their taxes are being paid. On the other hand, there is this other group of people who do not want to be anybody's employee. They want to take care of their own career, and they want to pay their own taxes.

Unfortunately, it's hard for a startup company to understand all the regulatory issues such as sales tax, income tax, payroll tax, workers' comp, and local taxes. Large companies usually have their own accounting department, or will use a PEO. The good news is that online marketplaces and compliance companies typically help both the company and the independent contractor stay within the legal bounds. [10]

Keeping It Legal

A number of drivers contribute to whether a company should bring on an individual as an independent contractor or an employee for the business to remain compliant. The use of independent contractors by private industry has been in place for decades through temp agencies, which offer companies the flexibility and ease of a non-employee-based workforce while remaining compliant. As the need for a more independent and flexible workforce increases, so will options for recruiting, selecting, and engaging this workforce beyond traditional temp agencies; hence, the rise of the human cloud and online marketplaces.

Insurance

As an independent consultant/interim executive, you are engaged by your clients to help them solve difficult problems. While all of these business relationships start off well, you cannot predict what you will encounter and whether engagements will end as amicably as they started. Business insurance is one option when you are looking to protect yourself from the unpredictable. In today's litigious world, it is risky to be without some kind of insurance; you never know when someone will sue you.

We worked with an executive who really didn't want to

---

[10] From presentation by Gene Zaino at Cerius Symposium, Talent Management in the 21st Century, October 10, 2014.

buy insurance because he had never needed it in the past. But we require all of our executives to have it as a prerequisite to engaging with one of our clients. We referred him to a few good sources we had used before and he bought from one of them. Fast-forward six months, and his own client he had just completed work for decided to sue him. In reality, it was considered a frivolous lawsuit. The owners made some decisions that had a negative impact on the company. Not wanting to accept responsibility, however, they tried to shift responsibility and accountability to the interim CFO. Regardless of how frivolous, fighting the claims would have likely have bankrupted the executive. His insurance covered the lawsuit and he was able to continue with his business knowing he had made the right decision to get insurance, even though originally, he had thought it wasn't necessary.

The only other comment we will make about insurance is advice given to us from our attorney at one point: "People typically don't sue for good reason; they sue out of desperation." As much as you vet and hand-pick your clients, make sure you are protected. Fighting one frivolous lawsuit could leave you bankrupt.

If you are serious about being an independent executive, don't risk your livelihood for the small annual cost of insurance. Look at it the same way you do car insurance or property insurance. It's just a necessary evil in today's litigious climate.

While there are many small business insurance products, these are the more common types recommended for independent executive businesses or listed as requirements by a client as part of a vendor agreement.

- **General Liability Insurance**

  The policy provides both defense and damages if a business owner, employees, products, or services cause or are alleged to have caused bodily injury or property damage to a third party. This is also called commercial general liability insurance. It is often applied or used to cover the following scenarios:

  - **Interacting with clients face-to-face:** If you visit a client's place of work or clients visit yours
  - **Having access to a client's equipment:** For example, IT professionals are covered against potential claims with IT business liability insurance
  - **Representing your client's business**
  - **Using third-party locations** for any business-related activities
  - **Meeting a requirement** to have general liability insurance before entering into a contract

  Some examples of what could be covered are below:

  - **Bodily injury:** A client falls over your bag and you are legally liable for the injury. This policy will cover the subsequent claim and related medical expenses up to your general liability policy's limits of liability.
  - **Property damage and data loss:** You spill coffee on a client's server, causing damage and

loss of data. This policy will cover the subsequent claim up to your general liability policy's limits of liability.

- **Personal injury:** One of your employees is at lunch. He talks to the owner of the shop about one of your clients in a false and unflattering way. The client learns of this discussion and sues for slander. This policy covers the subsequent claim, up to your general liability policy's limits of liability, and will pay for an attorney to defend you if necessary.

General liability insurance will not protect you from everything. For example, general liability will not cover you against claims of negligence, even if it isn't you or your business' fault.

- **Professional Liability Insurance:** This is also known as Errors and Omissions Insurance. The policy provides defense and damages for failure to perform or improperly rendering professional services. A general liability policy does not provide this protection, so it is important to understand the difference.
  - For a professional services business, having errors and omissions insurance coverage can be an integral part of protecting the business. Accusations of negligence or the failure to perform the professional services are things for which any professional services business can be sued for, even if it hasn't made a mistake or is

at fault. Errors and omissions coverage is most useful for businesses that provide a professional service or regularly give advice.

Some examples of what could be covered are below:

- **Protection even if you haven't made a mistake:** You advise a client to change some internal processes to increase productivity. The recommendations aren't implemented as you specified, and productivity subsequently drops by 15 percent rather than improving. Or if you manage the development of a new product. There are problems with the project (which are beyond your control) and you cannot deliver the final product in a timely manner, so your client sues you.

- **Negligent acts:** You advise a client to update their employment practices. Six months later, your client contacts you, stating a part-time employee is suing the company. You left out a key requirement about the number of hours that part-time employees are permitted to work, so your client sues you.

• **Business Owner's Policy (BOP):** This is a combination of general liability and business property insurance. BOP insurance is often used to provide balanced coverage for small businesses who also want to protect their own business equipment.

- **General liability insurance** protects your business from another person or business' claims of bodily injury, associated medical costs, and damage to their property.

- **Property Liability Insurance** protects your business furniture and equipment at up to five different office locations, which includes accidental damage.

Some examples of what could be covered are below:

- Office insurance for fire and business interruption
- Electronic data loss insurance
- Hired or non-owned vehicle liability insurance
- Commercial crime insurance to cover the dishonesty of your employees

Insurances for Employees Beyond Yourself

- **Commercial Auto Insurance:** If a business does not have company vehicles, but employees drive their own cars on company business, there is non-owned auto liability to protect the company in case the employee does not have insurance or has inadequate coverage. Many times, the non-owned policy can be added to the BOP policy.

- **Workers' Compensation:** Worker's compensation provides insurance to employees who are injured on the job. This type of insurance provides wage replacement and medical benefits to those who are injured while working. In exchange for these benefits, the employee gives up his or her rights to sue the employer for the incident. Such insurance protects the owner and the company from legal complications.

State laws will vary, but all require a business to have workers' compensation if there are W-2 employees besides the owner(s).

Insurance Requirements

Many large corporations may require you to carry a certain level of insurance in various categories. Based on what the client is requesting, this may be a good time to consider some type of intermediary that does cover all requirements and/or may already have a contract and vendor certification set up with the company.

Contracts and Attorneys

Beyond the SOW, there will be key points you will want to include in your terms and conditions for legal purposes. Again, we are not attorneys and are not providing legal advice. We advise that you speak with an attorney to get appropriate advice for your situation. This may also vary by state. Some executives have worked for years without a contract, while others have spent thousands on attorney fees putting one into place. Either way, at one point or another, you will likely end up needing to review and execute a client's contract. Here are a few of the top areas to focus on.

Confidentiality and Nondisclosure Agreements

At the very least, there will likely be some type of confidentiality agreement, (also known as a Nondisclosure Agreement). Although the law of ethics and integrity dictates that information shared between you and the client is confidential, some clients feel a little better having it in writing. You also may have information that you prefer to remain confidential. Every once in a while, we have come across an executive with a background in the venture capital and investment community who has a blanket policy not to sign these. Their reasoning has to do with raising capital and is not typically applicable when working as an independent executive.

Intellectual Property

You probably have built up some proprietary information and tools and will be using them during your engagement. They are intended for the use of the company within the parameters of the engagement only. You don't want any confusion about ownership of your tools. The engagement includes the use of them, not transfer of ownership. Are there any parameters of extended use or other application? What permissions are needed? Make sure you protect your proprietary information or intellectual property (IP) in the contract you sign, whether it's your agreement or the client's agreement.

Exclusivity

This pertains more to contracts with intermediaries or other business owners you may partner with. Does your involvement require you to secure business only through that entity, regardless of the lead source? For example, you have a colleague you worked with years ago, who has reached out and is referring you to one of his or her clients. Is this now your client, or is it the intermediary's or joint venture's client? Does your revenue-share agreement apply? An exclusivity agreement is only between you and your intermediary, not you and the client.

Non-compete

Although these may be common at the executive level with employment contracts, we do not see them in client-vendor contracts. Any concerns that may otherwise be covered by this type of clause is usually covered as part of the confidentiality and non-disclosure agreement.

Non-circumvention

This is very common with intermediary and online marketplace contracts and/or Terms of Use. These companies invest heavily in their systems, their networks, and their marketing. While you may not see the expense or time that went into your specific client connection, the client connection would not exist without all of that investment. If you are uncomfortable with the value of the revenue share or fees, that is a decision to be made at the time of initial sign-up. From that point on, let your ethics and integrity be your guide.

Indemnification

This is common in vendor contracts, whether it is with an intermediary or a client. It makes clear to both parties who is ultimately responsible for issues and costs arising from errors. In client contracts, a mutual indemnification up to the amount paid to the vendor is most common. When working with an intermediary, you will typically be asked to indemnify the intermediary. Once you are connected with the client, the intermediary is neither directly involved with nor in control of you or the client in your activities and actions. Since there is no participation, it is difficult to argue in favor of holding them responsible for any errors the vendor or client make.

Entities That Protect Your Assets

Working independently as a business owner does come with some additional responsibility and risks. Understand the tax liabilities, the laws, and the risks based on your services, your situation, and the state(s) you are doing business in. A decade ago, it was not uncommon for an executive to simply "hang out their shingle" and they were in business. Laws have changed, and the government is having a tough time properly classifying independent contractors. Consider seeking out professional advice on the type of entity that is best for you, including types and tax implications. Some common entity types are:

- Sole Proprietor
- LLC (Limited Liability Corporation)
- C Corporation
- S Corporation
- LLP (Limited Liability Partnership)

Pulling It All Together

Again, we are not certified experts in any of these areas. Hopefully, this chapter has offered enough base information for you to understand what certified experts you need to consult for your particular situation and know what initial questions to ask.

YOUR BUSINESS COACH

1. Do you want or need to protect your personal assets?

2. Do you understand the local and state independent compliance laws enough to ensure you are complying with them?

3. What type of insurance makes sense for your services and situation?

4. Do you have the resources and requirements to comply with large company vendor contracts, or do you need to team up or work through someone who does?

5. Have you talked with your CPA to determine the best entity structure for you?

CHAPTER 8

Delivering on Expectations

Managing the Engagement End-to-End

An independent executive is continually juggling various client demands, managing expectations, and doing the right thing for all stakeholders. It can be challenging to stay focused on why he or she was brought in to begin with and keep everyone on the same page and the right track. Here are a few things to remember as you balance priorities to make a lasting impact with your clients.

Communication

An organization cannot operate well without good communication. The same goes for an independent executive engagement. The biggest mistake an executive can make is taking for granted that, because they are continually talking and e-mailing with the client, the client is receiving proper communication regarding progress. Keep these communications separate and as simple and clear as can be. Create a basic SOW progress communication in a format that works best for you and the client. Here are some basic elements to include:

- SOW Goals

- Related Key Deliverables
- Target Date for Completion
- Percent Complete
- Dependencies (if any)
- Status and Concerns
- Additional Scope Added

If you or the client find colors helpful, color-code the items that are in progress with the traditional red (in trouble, on hold), yellow (have concerns, bottlenecked, behind schedule) or green (on track). Once the template is set up, it should take no more than five to ten minutes to update on a weekly, biweekly, or monthly basis. Your progress updates may vary depending on the amount of time you spend with the client. For example, if you are working with the client three to four days per week, consider reporting weekly. If your time commitment is two days per month, monthly makes more sense. We have seen some executives communicate weekly even if they worked just two hours that week. It keeps the SOW items and the executive top-of-mind and the client feeling informed about progress.

As easy as it is to hit "send" and be done with the update, schedule time with the client at regular intervals to talk through it. Don't expect that the client is opening, reading, and absorbing those e-mails; in most cases, they aren't.

Expectation Management

Some of the biggest complaints from companies are that consultants "didn't do the job they were brought in for," or "didn't accomplish what I expected them to do," or "didn't meet my expectations." Often, this cannot be further from reality, but the executive failed to clarify expectations at the beginning and/or stay consistent throughout the engagement. It is easy to get sidetracked with additional expectations because independent executives are often brought into disruptive situations.

In reality, circumstances may not allow the executive to achieve the expectations within a certain timeframe or at a specified level. Get all the information you need before you make any commitment; under-promise, over-deliver, and be very clear about what is expected. Though expectation management seems like an old business school term, we hear about the reality of mismanaged expectations when we have conversations with clients. And when they're happy with someone that they've hired in the past, it is rarely because they simply liked the person. It is because that person met their expectations.

How does an executive manage client expectations, especially when initial expectations are unrealistic? The biggest challenge is that those expectations are deeply rooted. They were formed the moment the client realized they had an issue or created a goal. Expectations about how to fix or achieve things predate any conversations they have with the executive, and initial conversations and the SOW are just a continuation of that.

The reality is that expectations also never really end. Relate it to remodeling a room in your house. Did your buying process start when you first stood in a showroom and started deciding on what fixtures you wanted? No. It started the moment you became dissatisfied with the current state of the room. That led to the decision to remodel. Then you went to a showroom to pick out fixtures. It also didn't end when you completed final sign-off on the contractor's paperwork accepting the job as complete. It continues every time you pass by or step into that room. Does the new room make you feel good? Are there different color choices you wish you had made? Have you started to notice flaws in the contractor's work? Client expectations are some of the most challenging elements of an engagement. Whatever the executive accomplishes doesn't have to have a big impact, as long as it is in line with the client's expectations and can result in a positive, lasting impact.

The communication process and template outlined above can help greatly. During conversations, expand your discussion beyond what was on the SOW. Have additional expectations unknowingly arisen? We see this quite a bit when following up with both executives and clients during engagements. One of two things can easily happen. Either the executive is so focused on the SOW they don't stop and listen to the client, or they get so sidetracked with additional requests and scope, they forget the SOW. Proper communication and staying focused on the client's expectations and the current situation can help make every engagement a successful one.

Leading as an Independent Executive

Leaders have different management styles and expectations, but what works for some might not work for others. An executive's chances for success depend on multiple factors, including their personality, past experiences, why they're being brought in, and the type of project they're working on.

Because of the temporary and dynamic nature of their work, independent executives need to be flexible in their leadership style. They need to switch styles to manage client expectations as well as get the job done. This may require varying styles within the same company, depending on the culture, individual personalities, and what needs to be accomplished.

Vary Your Approach to Fit the Situation

Independent executives are often brought in specifically to help change or form a leadership process in the organization. Because they're brought in to fill a role temporarily and at a time of change, there's a lot of inconsistency. The independent executive's primary purpose is to bring consistency to the situation. This can often be a challenge because many people are resistant to change; the executive needs to adjust accordingly.

Sometimes you may feel like Dr. Jekyll and Mr. Hyde, with multiple personalities on a given day, depending on what situation you're in, which company you're in, what the culture is, and with whom you're working throughout the organization. There isn't a black-and-white line among the various personalities and work styles. Sometimes it is a subtle difference. These subtle differences can either help to rebuild or cause additional turmoil in a company.

Matching Leadership Style to a Situation

There are great assessment tools to help you match your leadership style to a situation. These don't zero in on the exact personality of leaders but instead describe their work style.

Two executives may have the exact same skill set and knowledge, but how they address the situation, how they work within it, and their approaches can make one successful and the other fail. Matching the executive's leadership style with the company's culture, executive team, CEO, and situation is key.

For example, if the CEO of a growing company is accustomed to doing most things him- or herself, it is sometimes difficult to transition the work and trust others to do it thoroughly and well. The result is a period of micromanagement. If we are placing a part-time executive in a CFO role to work with this CEO, we will look for one who works well with micromanagers and can be patient, understanding, and communicate well through the transition. Not every executive works well in that kind of environment. Understanding your work style and what the client needs or expects can be critical.

Striking the Right Balance

According to the University of San Diego, leadership can be categorized into three kinds of interpersonal behaviors:

aggressive, nonassertive, and assertive. Aggressive leaders humiliate employees and get what they want at the expense of others. Nonassertive leaders do not express their ideas and wants and as a result often do not get what they want, resulting in pent-up anger and resentment. Assertive leaders stand up for their ideas in ways that do not violate the rights of others, creating respect between themselves and their subordinates. The last kind of leader strikes the right balance by often getting what they want and at the same time feeling good, valued, and respected in the workplace. (Source: http://www.sandiego.edu/student-leadership/documents/3%20 types%20interpersonal.pdf)

One of the many abilities of effective leaders is to be aggressive when the situation demands it, or assertive as needed. They switch according to the demands of the situation. But executives who leave a permanent position in an organization for an interim one have to learn to play the field according to the client's expectations. It's a big change for them to no longer be in charge and align with what that CEO or board requires.

Leaving Your Expertise Behind

One of our favorite sayings is, "I worked myself out of a job." This should be your top goal. Whether you are brought in to bridge a gap, put processes in place, or lend your expertise to a situation, much of what you do and how you do it should be left behind when you leave. The organization should have all the information they need to continue on as though you were still there. It is no different than how you would advise an entrepreneur starting a business. Start with your exit and work backward. From the first meeting with the client, be thinking about how you will accomplish what is needed and how you will exit while making what you did stick with the team left in place.

Your communication, your toolkit, and your interactions should work in unison to support this goal. If you are providing knowledge, put it in writing and explain as much of the reasoning behind it as possible. Work one-on-one with individuals you know have the aptitude to thrive in the organization, or help the client hire someone from the outside who can do the job. Sometimes the organization just needs structure or processes in order to improve on their own when things start to go wrong. Walk them through the process; have them do as much of it on their own as they can, and then step back and support.

Engagements typically go through a pattern of time involvement with interim executives. At the beginning, most of your time will be spent gathering information and planning. During the execution phase, the executive's involvement will even out, and finally slow down as the engagement reaches completion. Using a five-days-a-week interim engagement as an example: The executive walks into a turnaround situation and works five-plus days per week at the start. The executive spends most of his or her time answering questions, assessing, planning, and putting out fires. As planning turns into execution and training begins, a point will come when the executive can reduce time on-site to three days per week. This gives the internal team a couple of days without the executive to rely on. As the team starts to thrive and operate as the plan intended, the executive is there perhaps only one day a week to focus in on remaining open items. Progress will not stop once the executive leaves; the team is equipped for the current stage of growth and the path that has been laid out for them.

When the Engagement Starts to Veer from the SOW

Since everything was documented to begin with and you are tracking your progress through updates and reporting, any significant variance should become clear quickly. If you are adding more to the "added activities" list than you are updating on the progress, or if most SOW items are in the yellow or red zone due to some internal issues, decision makers, available resources, etc., those are red flags.

We have mentioned this a number of times in this chapter. Why? It happens too often and too easily.

Clients are thrilled to not only have someone of your expertise working with them, but also someone to talk to and confide in. The more you work with clients, the more they will realize you can help in areas other than those outlined in the original Statement of Work. You may be happy to help in any way you can and keep saying, "Sure, I can do that for you." There is nothing wrong with this impulse, other than that many times, the client may expect these additional items to also be included within the original budget or timelines, and that can easily distract you from focusing on the original deliverables. As long as it is all in writing and you are discussing it with the client, you will be able to keep up with adjusting the client's expectations. You have the choice of either expanding the SOW or putting off the additional items until the original scope of work is completed. Part of the role you will end up playing is an advisor.

Measuring, Tracking, and Results—The Impact

Quite a bit can be accomplished during an engagement. Measuring and tracking the results and impact of your efforts is important and very little says it better than numbers. Keeping track of what you achieved, both qualitatively and quantitatively, can help keep everything in perspective. Refer back to Chapter 5 for more detail and some examples if needed.

Pulling It All Together

Clients can be your best advocates in the marketplace with referrals and repeat business. Take the time to communicate, stay on the same page, and do the right thing for your clients. It can either come back to help you in dividends or haunt you.

YOUR BUSINESS COACH

1. What communication tools are you using with clients to keep them updated on progress toward the SOW?

2. How are you measuring and tracking your results and accomplishments with your client?

3. Are you regularly checking with your client to ensure expectations are aligned and being met?

4. Do you adjust your leadership style to various clients and their teams?

5. Are you working with the internal team to leave behind as much of your expertise as possible with the company upon completion of your engagement?

6. Do you have an initial plan with each client to handle intended or unintended adjustments to the original scope?

SECTION III

Leveraging Initial Success

CHAPTER 9

Make Money While You Sleep

Referral Fees

Each independent executive has his or her own policy on referral fees. Some see it as a good business practice to not accept any referral fees, for any number of reasons (the most popular is that they don't want to be seen by their network as referring someone just because they receive a referral fee). More times than not though, we do see referral fee arrangements within the community. Referral fees between individuals usually range from 5–20 percent, with 10 percent being the average.

As you build your client portfolio, you are likely to come in contact with a number of opportunities for which you are not the right fit but know someone who is. You decide whether referral fees from other executives is an added revenue source for your business or not. We have seen a number of executives build a substantial base of business through referring out business.

Putting a Value on Your Tool Kit

The old saying, "One man's trash is another man's treasure," is a good way of looking at some of the everyday, common-sense tools you use. As basic as they may seem to you, they may be invaluable to someone else. Think about how fundamental a meeting agenda template and guidelines for effective meetings are. We have seen these basic tools shift small businesses and start a transformation process.

Think about an interim marketing executive working with a client. One of the key things the executive needs to know is the marketing budget. But the client has never put together a budget. As much as the next step should be for the client to bring in a finance executive to do a budget, that likely won't happen in the near-term. The marketing executive could spend some time creating a template, but it doesn't make sense to do so on his or her own time, nor for the client to pay a marketing executive to create a budgeting template. In these circumstances, we have seen executives reach out to their network or go online and secure a template. Even though there is a cost in some instances, it is much lower than creating one from scratch.

— CASE IN POINT —

Turning a One-Pager into Profits

Marc Koehler has been an independent executive for about fifteen years. The twelve years prior to that were with Fortune 100 companies such as Honeywell and Siemens, and as a submarine officer for the United States Navy. It was quite a transition going from the Navy to large corporations. On a submarine, when you say you are going to get underway at 1300, you didn't get underway at 1259, and you didn't get underway at 1301; you got underway at 1300. It was all about getting the mission done. For Marc, it was a tough transition going to big companies where decisions take forever to make, you feel like one of many, and you don't feel like you're really making a big difference.

When he initially transitioned to being independent, there were some challenges. He found that when he went into small companies, they were all over the place. Everyone would just come to work, go into their cubicle or office, work, and then they'd leave. There was no sense of, "Hey, I'm going to work today with a great sense of purpose, and I left today with a great feeling of accomplishment." There was a big, gaping hole in all of these small businesses. And the hole was, with the speed of business today, it's not about a command-and-control style type of leadership; it's about a team delivering results. You create a team by helping people galvanize their own common purpose and a shared vision.

From that realization, Marc's brand began to formulate. He noticed the one big frustration these business owners had was hearing about best practices, but not being able to apply them inside their companies. Or if they tried, they wouldn't stick. He started by simplifying a lot of the tools and best practices that are used by big businesses.

Every single time he went into a company, he followed the "Marc Koehler Process." Eventually, his brand became a process-driven approach to helping a business owner create an engaged team. Once the team was engaged, he could focus everybody on the things that mattered most. Then he would make sure everybody was kept up to speed so that everybody on the team could help manage change and drive success.

To tell the story, he leveraged his background with the Navy. He compares a small business of 100 people to the same 100 people on a submarine. Why were they so engaged in the submarine? It was because everybody understood the big mission, and they understood their own role and everyone else's role. They use a lot of symbolism, such as flags, to reinforce these understandings. Marc translates this in small businesses through the use of his One-Page Strategic Plan. You can walk into any business that Marc works with and ask anyone what the mission of the company is. Instead of reciting word-for-word, they will say it in one word or point to a picture on the wall that they helped choose to represent the mission.

As he was working with these companies, often other consultants were also connected to the same companies. These others consultants looked at the one-page mission statement and said, "Hey, that's a really neat tool. Can I use that?" Obviously, Marc had no problem with that; he just asked that they leave his name and logo at the bottom of the page. The feedback he got when they used it was, "It was fantastic. It was great. Everybody's on the same page now. They're all focused and everybody understands the vision of the company."

That was Marc's real aha moment. He could have done turnarounds for the rest of his life, doing two or three of them a year and get paid pretty well. But he saw a greater opportunity in putting together the products and tools that he had used to help small businesses be more successful. He saw a great opportunity to take them, package them up, commercialize them, and then share the result with other business owners. He did this because he believed he would be able to reach more people and affect far more lives by showing them how to use these tools; basically, teaching them how to fish instead of fishing for them. It goes back to one of the core concepts of being an interim executive: you start with the end in mind, "How do I exit the company, and how do I make sure that everything I did sticks?" That was always his goal. That's how Marc started Lead with Purpose.

To commercialize it, he knew it had to be easily

accessible, easily updated, and scalable. He worked with a programmer and created it as an online platform available to companies and consultants/coaches working with companies via a subscription model.

Marc had the same thought process as many others: "Hey, I've built it, and they're going to come, and they're going to see it, and they're going to understand it." He was quickly reminded of a key learning. It's really important to know the small business owner. Marc says, "What we had to do is create that bridge so that when people signed in online, they would have all the support and tools they needed to build their own one-page plan, and they could build it on their own with their team. It was an interesting transition because there are all these other things you think are so easy for people to do. But if you stay really close to your client and the value that you want to provide them, and you keep getting feedback, it helps you to keep adjusting the offering."

That's what he did. He kept adjusting the offering and adding support, including videos, training sessions, etc. and finally started to gain some traction. Now, although they were solving one problem for their customers, they were creating another. They needed to focus on the support part of the product more than the product itself.

Through all of Marc's lessons learned, the top of the list would be to really know your customer. Pay attention to what they are saying. You only know that by saddling up next to them, understanding what their challenges are, and what their fears are. That's number one. Number two is, they're not going to automatically or easily translate that the tool or product that you have is going to help solve those fears, or help solve those problems. Make sure that everything communicates. Are you communicating in the simplest manner, so that people can understand? As much as you can, take out all the things that are non-value-added. You have to simplify. You have to connect how your tool or product is going to help make their life better for them. That was really big.

Pulling It All Together

One of the top rules of thumb any adviser would give a company is to diversify. Diversify your client base and your product/service offering. Never relying on just one product or source for your income can be critical when building a successful business. If you are just getting started, it may take some time, but always be thinking ahead about how you can diversify your revenue streams.

CHAPTER 10

How to Know if Partnering is Right for You

Why Independent Executives Partner

Partnering with other executives who are also building their independent executive business can lessen some of the challenges if you find the right partner(s).

Working on a more regular basis with other executives can provide the support and desire to be part of a team that tends to be human nature. As a company executive, you are used to a variety of interactions, relationships, strategic conversations, collaborative work with others who have complementary skill sets, and more. You lose some of that as an independent, beyond the clients you work with.

You also gain some complimentary skill sets to offer your clients. As you build your business with the right partner, he or she can bring in skills you do not have, allowing you to expand the number of services you can offer your clients.

Types of Partnerships

The arrangement you make can be as simple as a referral partnership or as formal as the formation of a legal partnership. The more common arrangement is somewhere in the middle. The executives share the same company name, meet on a regular basis, work together on business development, and split some shared costs, such as marketing.

Starting off with a referral partnership is a great way to test the waters and see how you work together. It can be structured, with regular meetings involving a handful of executives with varying expertise and a single target market. For example, an executive who works primarily with start-ups is not the best person for an ongoing referral arrangement if your target market is companies $20–$100 million in size. Some executives have a niche client base, whether by design or circumstance. Find out the details before extending the invitation; you never know where it may lead. Cerius started with a group of consultants who met weekly at a local restaurant. Through this informal partnership of referrals, they got to know each other's strengths. Some were great at finance and operations, while others had strengths in sales and IT.

A partnership doesn't need to be long-term. Sometimes, it may just be necessary for a particular engagement or client. Sometimes you will have great success, and other times, you may end up saying, "Never again."

Deciding Whether Partnership Is Right for You

Take it slowly and approach it as you would any other business relationship. Do your due diligence. Look for red flags indicating potential issues. Also, look for opportunities and how the situation can be leveraged for all involved.

If you decide it is a good idea, make sure you find the best match to your own values, goals, leadership style, and skills. Because once you become partners, it is vastly more difficult to undo the partnership than it was to create it.

Following are seven points to take into account to avoid a bad partnership.

1. Trust

This is first on the list for a reason. Bottom line: do you trust this individual with your personal bank account? If the answer is "no," think twice. As partners, every dollar you spend proportionately affects your own personal checkbook. There are a number of variations of partnerships in this industry. Find one that gives you the benefits you need, but perhaps doesn't involve the commingling of funds.

2. Friendship

If the person is a good friend, make sure that his or her goals, values, and responsibilities are aligned with yours. Don't assume that just because you get along as friends, they are. Take a look at the potential partner's personal life and how stable it is. Personal problems are difficult and can easily complicate somebody's professional life. If there is any doubt, don't do it.

3. Trial run

Select a person you have experience with at work, at a nonprofit, or on a project. You should know if he or she is a team player and how he or she reacts in difficult situations. If you have no experience with a potential partner at all, do a trial run for a specified period of time before finalizing the partnership.

4. Varied strengths

Make sure you and your partner's strengths are in different areas. If you have two people who are good at sales and no one who is good at executing on an operational level, it will be more challenging than you think. It is much better to bring someone in who will compliment your strengths. In order to grow profitably, keep some balance.

5. Balanced responsibilities

Both parties need to agree up front what their responsibilities are in the partnership and stick to them. If one person keeps trying to take over and do everything or ends up doing very little, then the partnership will start to unravel and feelings of resentment will fester.

6. Money

Just as in marriage, money is always one of the major potential problems in a business partnership. Therefore, agree in the beginning how you will use the funds you have and how the profits will be distributed.

7. List ownership

Decide up front how your lists will be owned, managed, and divided, from marketing lists to contacts to customer base. Have a plan for how these will be cultivated, respected, and divided should one partner decide to leave.

Why is all of this so important? Because a great business can be severely damaged by a bad partnership and never reach its full potential. Starting a business and/or a partnership is an emotional experience. When you are performing due diligence, set your emotions aside and make sure everything lines up and has the potential for staying aligned.

— CASE IN POINT —
Partnership Perspectives

For more than fifteen years, Gene Kaplan has been an independent executive and part of a success consortium, as he calls it. As a mechanical engineer, Gene always understood how things worked. As his career evolved, he learned how to make things work optimally. He worked as an engineer before starting his own systems integration company. After a shift in the marketplace and a change of client needs, Gene closed down his business and transitioned from being an entrepreneur to being a solopreneur. He saw it as a pretty easy transition and a soft landing because he was able to leverage all of his long-standing relationships in supply chain and manufacturing into client engagements for a growing independent executive business.

Some of those relationships were with people with whom he had worked inside his company or in the industry and who also wanted to be independent. They had been working together on projects here and there as well as referring business to each other. After a while, they decided to start getting a little more serious about it. They saw the need to better coordinate the group and pull in more people on larger projects. They have been focused on working with larger companies and contracts for about five years now and have been very successful at it. They are able to bring an array of expertise and perspective you would get from a large firm while offering the flexibility many clients appreciate. When they won a large contract against a well-known firm that was focused specifically on what the client was looking for and had even written books on it, Gene asked the question, "Why us?" The client said it was the flexibility in their offering, and the knowledge they weren't going to shove a standard program down the client's throats."

Gene says his consortium is made up of a group of seasoned executives with whom he has had prior dealings, who work well together, have similar cultures and philosophies, and can deliver a great product to clients, either individually or in teams. There is a core group of individuals, an additional network of expertise that is not needed as often, and partners who provide resources beyond professional services. For example, the consortium doesn't provide accounting services. It is not where the engagement focus is, but there are times on a project when clients need a good accounting or finance professional's advice. There's no formal agreement regarding referral fees nor a standard operating procedure. Each executive operates his or her own business, and each client situation is unique. It is up to each to do the right thing for the client and make it work when referring someone from within the consortium or when working as a team.

When asked by clients to explain why they operate as they do, Gene answers, "What's different about us is we're people working together because we want to, not because we happen to be employed by the same company."

Gene describes the consortium, "There is a lot of overlap on expertise, and we like that. Take one of our partners, who came out of one of our clients. He is an operations executive. He focuses on having regular meetings with clients and keeps moving the people and the project along. He has worked within these kinds of companies his whole career, whereas I never have. All of my experience is from the project side, as a service to the client. It's good that our group has both kinds of professionals because sometimes you need that project perspective from the outside, and sometimes you really need the perspective of someone who has walked in the client's shoes. We can do the same thing, but looking through different eyes."

When considering partnering with someone or a group, Gene offers a few things to consider: Am I just a small number in a really big crowd? Is this just another LinkedIn group and someone's taking some money? What are they going to do for me? Why do they need/want me? If they don't, it's a one-way street. Why am I important to them? Considering partnering with individuals who have overlapping skills, not just complementary ones. Don't try to be everything to everyone; develop your value discipline, and be able to clearly articulate it, both as a group and an individual.

Pulling It All Together

Partnering, formally or informally, with other individuals in a similar situation can offer executives the flexibility and independence that initially attracted them to this career while still retaining some benefits of being part of a team, including more collaboration, brainstorming, meaningful partner relationships, and any number of other opportunities to grow your businesses together.

CHAPTER 11

How to Maintain Momentum

Out of Sight, Out of Mind

It is commonly said that the best time to look for a job is when you currently have one. It is no different when building your business. This is one of the biggest pitfalls as you start to get work and are busy. Your business development efforts certainly will lessen, but do not put them on hold. The nature of independent executive work is that it is temporary. Continuing to work on lead sourcing will lessen the time lag between engagements, increase your ability to be more selective of the engagements you really want, and keep you top-of-mind throughout your network.

It is common for executives to put a hold on business development while working on engagements, then pick up efforts again when they are two to four weeks from the end of work. Their schedules are a little more open at that point. This can work well, depending on the length of each engagement. Remember, however, it doesn't take long for your sources to forget to refer you. It is also common for referral sources not to take the time to check on your availability and simply assume that you are too busy for new work.

Step back and think about how you would advise a client who says to you, "I'm too busy to bring in more business." You may need to get creative and adjust the focus of your efforts and a few of your tactics, but there is always some amount of time every week that can be devoted to building up your pipeline of opportunities.

Pay Attention: Identifying and Leveraging Opportunities

We have discussed this a number of times throughout this book. Think back to Jayne, Joanne, and Marc, who each were paying attention and found ways to uniquely leverage what they had discovered into incredible opportunities to create and grow their independent executive businesses.

Jayne could have easily simply attended her professional conference and continued to apply it to her existing profession. Instead, she saw the opportunity to blend her background as a speech-language pathologist and combine it with working in the business world.

For Joanne, "pay attention" became a mantra as she leveraged opportunities like rungs of a ladder in the process of creating a highly-specialized business teaching others how to get more referrals.

Finally, Marc paid attention to everyone, from his customers to other executives to his referral partners, and created a growing technology platform to more easily deliver his services. He not only created a product but also monetized his toolkit.

Instead of instinctually saying, "that wouldn't work for me," pay attention and adopt the perspective, "how do I make that work for me?"

Write the Book on It

Of course, you can always end up writing a book on your experiences and expertise. With the ease of self-publishing and e-books, this is becoming more popular. Rather than beginning with the subject you want to write about, start with your target audience in mind. As counterintuitive as it may seem, your main goal for writing a book is not necessarily to be a bestseller or an expectation that it will change the lives of thousands. The goal is to enhance your other marketing and business development efforts. Rather than asking, "who would buy my book?" to select your target audience, think along the lines of, "which audience(s) do I want to speak in front of?" The answer to that question is your target audience. Now work backwards through topics that would be interesting and useful as a presentation, webinar, or speaker series. From there, we strongly recommend you work with an expert who can guide you through the outline, compilation, completion, and publishing process. There are a number of great sources out there who work exclusively with consultants writing books specifically for the purpose of marketing their services. If you have never written so much as an article in your life, you may want to have a ghostwriter write your book for you.

One of the biggest frustrations for independent executives is the challenge of getting in front of potential clients. Many of them are not out at the networking events. They are sitting at their desks, networking, or traveling. They are, however, large consumers of information. Give them something to read on their next flight.

— CASE IN POINT —
Writing Everyone's Book on It

As part of his exit strategy from his advertising and public relations agency, Henry DeVries combined his love of writing and his desire to help teach consultants and coaches the science of attracting clients. Over a period of eight years, he invested significantly and tied in with Harvard Business School to scientifically research how to attract clients. His research revealed a proven way for independent executives to obtain a marketing return-on-investment of 400 percent to 2000 percent—write the book on it.

Henry founded Indie Books International and now focuses his efforts on helping independent consultants, coaches, and business owners with the preparation, publication, and promotion of a book that grows their businesses, puts money in the bank, and helps them make the difference they want to make. As Henry puts it, "We educate consultants and coaches that the publication of the book is the starting line, not the finish line."

According to David H. Maister, a professor from the Harvard Business School who wrote *Managing the Professional Service Firm*, the typical sales and marketing hype that works for retailers and manufacturers is not only a waste of time and money for independent executives; it actually makes them less attractive to prospective clients.

"The number one challenge for independent executives is creating new clients," says Henry. "Ironically, many independent executives feel marketing is too time-consuming, expensive, or undignified. Even if they try a marketing or business development program, most are frustrated by a lack of results. They even worry about whether marketing would ever work for them."

According to Henry's research, the best approach for independent executives is to demonstrate expertise by sharing valuable information through writing and speaking. "This I believe in my heart of hearts," says Henry. "The number one marketing tool is a book, and the number one marketing strategy is a speech. Research shows independent executives can fill a pipeline with qualified prospects in as little as thirty days by offering advice to prospects on how to overcome their most pressing problems."

CHAPTER 12

Parting Words

Have a Passion for What You Do

Regardless of why you started down this path or are considering it, don't forget to keep aligned with what you are passionate about. This starts with your brand, continues in your communications, and is seen throughout your interactions with customers and your network. The more authentic you are, the more others will build trust with you. If you aren't excited about what you do and how you can help, you can't expect others to be. The more passion you have for what you do, the more it will conjure the same passion and excitement in others.

Do the Right Thing

This includes for your customers, your network, your family, and you. Set your guiding principles and, when in question, do the right thing. Replace the Golden Rule with the Platinum Rule, "Do unto others as they would have you do unto them." Your interactions should be reflective of the preferences of those around you, not necessarily as you believe it should be. We have seen too many bridges burned from this. Although you may not ask for a referral fee when you refer business to another executive, respect others if they do have a policy of accepting referrals. Understand their preferences and parameters and respect them. If you are referred a client and you know someone who is likely a better fit, let the referral source know and make the introduction. Only take the engagement if you know you can make an impact and provide value. When you make an engagement about money in the short-term, it doesn't take long for it to jeopardize you long-term.

Help Yourself by Helping Others

It is said that one of the qualities of great salespeople is their ability to not get discouraged. You will encounter a range of "No, thank you," "I just referred business to someone, I wish we had gotten together yesterday," those who don't bother to respond to you at all, and everything in between. Building your business, your brand, and your reputation can take time. Step back and think about what you would advise a business owner coming to you asking, "How long will it take for you to make an impact on my company or turn it around?" And be careful not to get caught up in the "it's all about me, give me business," vortex. The more you focus on others and how you can help them, the more willing they will be to help you.

We have been incredibly blessed by the gracious giving and help of our network. Please don't miss an opportunity to help someone. A great ending statement to any conversation is, "What can I do for you?" It's such a simple sentence, yet it can be so powerful, particularly when you mean it. We have seen too many people in our business make everything all about them. It is those who make it about helping others, with no expectation of anything in return, who end up with the most success.

For more resources visit www.howifiredmyboss.com.

About the Authors

Kristen McAlister joined Pamela Wasley to purchase Cerius. She has spent most of her career helping companies establish and improve their infrastructure for high growth. She has grown companies and created optimal infrastructure from both an operational and client management perspective. Kristen has spent the last ten years teaching companies how to leverage executives for transitional situations such as high growth and turnarounds. She is a national speaker and is published on topics ranging from operations and productivity to talent management and the contingent workforce. Kristen is a mother, Ironman, and Marine wife.

Pamela Wasley is one of the founders and CEO of Cerius. She is a serial entrepreneur who has personally sold two companies and led a management buyout of Cerius. She has advised hundreds of companies on strategies for growth and higher shareholder value, served on several private boards, and is a frequent national speaker and is published on the topics of mergers and acquisitions, the workforce of the future, and global contingent workforces.

ACKNOWLEDGMENTS

We want to thank our families, who support us no matter the path we take. For this, we are grateful.

We especially want to acknowledge our special contributors whose daily experiences and input helped complete this book: Heather, Maria, and Matt.

Made in the USA
San Bernardino, CA
19 March 2017